"Shak doesn't sacrifice the detail; he just has a great way of making the complicated easy to understand."

Charles Proctor
Presbyterian Deacon
proud cancer survivor

"Shak Hill's book is an excellent, easy to read and understand financial road map for any individual or family facing a life threatening diagnosis."

Rich Santos
Group Publisher
Wealth Management Group
Penton Media, Inc.

Also by Shak Hill

A Woman's Guide to Financial Planning:
The Seven Essential Ingredients For Your Best Financial Recipe

WHEN THE DOCTOR SAYS IT'S CANCER

OR ANY OTHER LIFE THREATENING DIAGNOSIS

A CARING FINANCIAL PLAN FOR LIFE

SHAK HILL

Robak, LLC
Centreville, VA

WHEN THE DOCTOR SAYS IT'S CANCER
A Caring Financial Plan For Life

Robak, LLC books may be ordered through booksellers or by contacting:
Robak, LLC
6501 Flowerdew Hundred Court
Centreville, VA 20120
www.YourFinancialGuidingLight.com

Because of the dynamic nature of the Internet, any Web addresses or links contained in this book may have changed since publication and may no longer be valid. The views expressed in this work are solely those of the author and do not necessarily reflect the views of the publisher, and the publisher hereby disclaims any responsibility for them.

ISBN: 978-0-9841334-0-6

Printed in the United States of America

Robak LLC rev. date: 5/7/2010

CONTACT SHAK
To book Shak for your events or
For more information and to order your signed copy, go to
www.YourFinancialGuidingLight.com
Robak@YourFinancialGuidingLight.com

Your Financial Guiding Light™

This book is dedicated to all who keep hope alive,
especially my precious Robin.

CONTENTS

Acknowledgements

I had just finished my first book when my wife Robin said to me, "You know, Shak, those diagnosed with cancer need financial planning."

That did it.

I guess I have one of those minds that when an idea enters and it feels right, watch out. The burners, no the *after-burners* kick in; I get moving, I don't stop for much. Like any effort, many are involved to help make it a reality. This effort is no different.

If you could ever find a mentor and friend better than Charlie Settgast, then you are truly blessed. This makes me truly blessed with his candidness and expertise. Thank you, Charlie for your tireless contributions that will allow this work to help others.

Attorney Laura Possessky (www.gurapossessky.com) and Attorney William Kovatch, Jr. (www.kovatchelderlaw.com) both gave key insight to some of the legal concepts. Frank Stitely, CPA, (www.skcpas.com) helped focus my thoughts. Pat Kashtock really came through helping me become more active and clear. Maida Lanstein brought it down to earth.

If you need a web master, contact Tyler Bamberg (www. sdcfm.biz). Nice job. For the second project in a row, Mike Powell of Greenroom Recording (www.greenroomrecording.com) patiently let me read and reread the book into audio. Your detail and professionalism shows through. Tess Stockslager helped with the academic look and sharpened my pen.

Rebecca Patton, Allison Scoles, Gwyn Kennedy Snider (gkscreative.com), Suzan Tugberk, Kathleen Hill, and Le-Ha Anderson all helped with the design and beauty of this book. Thank you Meghan Codd of Zuula Consulting (www. zuulaconsulting.com) for your belief in this project. Donna Pagano, CFP®, thank you for your encouragement and vision (www.FamilyLoveLetter.com).

Greg Clough of Arlington Benefits Group (www.arlbenefits.com) helped with his knowledge of the benefits available in the work place. Thank you.

To all caregivers, especially my brother, Rev. Peter Mangum, for the cross-country ride and baptism and Robin's sister, Debbie Ricci, for finding the right doctors, your tireless compassion is very much appreciated.

I want to acknowledge you. I hope you live while alive and I hope you dance as often as you can. Despite the diagnosis, move forward with life. I truly hope this book helps.

Preface

"*It's cancer*" – those two words conjure up feelings of despair, fear, anxiety and sadness. The mind races trying to imagine what this means about physical well-being, mental health, faith, life, death, family and legacy.

My wife, Robin, and I heard these words in 1992. The thought of losing her, witnessing her fight to survive and the ensuing successful battle with the disease shaped my life and brought Robin and I closer than we had ever been before.

During Robin's fight, I journeyed from an Air Force pilot to a financial planner. Both the journey and the battle changed my perspective on life. After that time of worry, pain and confusion ended, I realized we had neglected large parts of our world. We didn't have a will, estate planning documents, or even a health care directive. We didn't review our financial accounts or look at the beneficiaries. We didn't pay attention to the fact that significant tax advantages and estate planning techniques are available, saving angst and countless headaches, let alone potentially thousands of dollars needlessly going to the tax man or the probate process. *Moreover*, what's worse, not one person suggested we even consider how cancer influences this part of our lives.

While looking at the available help for individuals and families battling a life threatening diagnosis, I realized very little guidance is offered on how your financial life will be affected. I have written this book so you don't make the mistakes we almost made. Perhaps, like us many years ago, you don't have someone to help you prepare your finances for life both during and after your diagnosis. This book will provide you the tools to understand and deal with them effectively.

I hope that your outcome will be as glorious as ours has been, but no matter your ultimate outcome, you will need to make important decisions, and make them soon. Though life changes completely when the doctor says it's cancer, your financial ship should not drift unattended.

You have to live while alive. I hope you take every opportunity to enjoy life and all that it has to offer. I hope that you learn how to play the guitar, learn the foreign language you always wanted to learn, travel to your grandchildren or to that desired destination. I hope you dance.

At the same time, your legacy demands you attend to many important financial matters.

I hope my personal experience and professional insight can help guide you.

The first step is not to panic. You cannot wish away or deny what is happening in your life. If you do, this will only work to complicate your task.

The second step is to consider your legacy and the life lessons you want to leave behind. Within this legacy step, you decide how to handle the finances and the transition of your affairs to your loved ones. With modern medical advances, your diagnosis is not an automatic death sentence. One part of your fight is medical and another, often overlooked part is financial. Use this diagnosis as a wake up call to care for important family needs. Now is the time to build your legacy by getting your financial house in order.

The third step is to fight as hard as you can. I sincerely hope your story ends as pleasant as mine has. However, no matter the outcome, by taking these important steps, you will have long-term positive consequences all the way around.

I have been there. Let this book help.

1

Our Personal Story

When I was growing up, my mother always said to tell her the end first, *then* give her the details when updating her on an important event in my life. For example, when I was in high school, I got into a fender bender with another car. Due to wet, rainy conditions, my simple stop at a light became a five-miles-an-hour hydroplaning glide into the car in front of me. When I called my mother from a pay phone and said I was in an accident, she nearly lost her mind.

"First, you should have told me you were all right," she shouted, "*then* told me you were in an accident!"

Years later, in pilot training with the United States Air Force, I told her, "Tomorrow, I am going to fly solo for the first time!" The flight went well, and I called her soon thereafter to share the good news.

Rather than offering praise or excitement, she said, "Next time, just tell me you went solo after you are safely on the ground!" She confessed to me years later that the day before my first solo flight, she was worrying all night long. She was scared to death!

It only took a *few* more experiences before I understood the importance of the way information is shared, but I've learned my lesson. So, before I tell you the personal story of why I came to write this book, let me begin by telling you the uplifting way it *ends*.

The End

Today, my wife, Robin, enjoys great health. She is a vibrant, seventeen-year cancer survivor and she and our son, Jake, are doing great (other than the fact that at 17, he seems to have misplaced his brain, like all growing, normal teenage males tend to do).

The Beginning

In 1992, Robin was pregnant with Jake, our second child. I enjoyed a successful direction in my career as the Air Force Academy invited me back to serve as an instructor pilot for the cadets. We just celebrated our daughter Sararose's first birthday and moved into our new home in Colorado. Life traveled on an exciting path for our growing family. With another baby on the way, we truly appreciated all of God's blessings.

Then, in the fourth month of pregnancy, Robin noticed discomfort in her left pelvic area. During normal prenatal checkups, she pointed this out and the doctors merely dismissed the complaint as regular maternal pains. The next month, however, she went back and informed them the pain had worsened.

With another baby on the way, we truly appreciated all of God's blessings.

"The baby must be sitting on the sciatic nerve," they told her. "It will go away after birth."

When Robin went to the following monthly checkup, the pain was not subsiding, but getting worse. The doctors believed she wasn't heeding their advice and was over-exerting herself in our new home. They started approaching Robin skeptically. No matter how much we tried to convince them of our concerns, the doctors wouldn't listen. So, we continued life as normal as possible, trying to overlook the pain. Although constantly uncomfortable, Robin began holiday decorating and prepared a delicious Thanksgiving meal.

With Christmas a month away, we enjoyed our newly constructed home overlooking the front range of the Colorado Rocky Mountains. With picturesque landscape views of Pike's Peak to the south and the Air Force Academy to the north, our house was beautiful and cozy. We could see the majesty of the Lord even better from our second-story bedroom window and from there, gaze at the world for hours.

We were excited and in awe.

Our postcard-perfect home would soon welcome our second child. My career rocketed forward. In addition to being an instructor pilot, I also head coached the Academy Prep School soccer team (the same team I had played on eight years earlier). With Christmas in the air, our home sparkled with decorations. All was well. Our future was bright.

Except for Robin's pain, life was good.

Just after Christmas, however, the pain intensified to the point where Robin could no longer walk without enduring crippling discomfort. Her only relief came from lying on her left side, the side of the pain and floating in the bathtub. (We would later understand why this was relaxing. In essence, while she floated in the tub, gravity released its hold, suspending the tumor for those brief moments.) Robin was up to eight baths a day.

Because she was pregnant, the doctors—understandably—did not perform normal diagnostic testing to uncover the source of her pain. Without any evidence to explain her symptoms, however, they labeled Robin a hypochondriac. Nevertheless we knew better than to believe the pain was a figment of her imagination.

After weeks of trying to convince her doctors to pay attention, they finally admitted Robin for supervised hospital care on January 2, 1993. But the doctors weren't fully on our side ... yet. They still believed the cause of pain was because Robin ignored their warnings and performed household chores, or because she did not correctly take her prescribed Tylenol with codeine.

A week later, (yes, it took a full week to get them to agree to further testing after I threatened to move her to a different hospital) they finally did an MRI and discovered "a mass" in her left pelvis. Talk about an attitude adjustment. We certainly don't blame the medical staff and although they never spoke the words, we could tell they were very sorry for having treated her with such disregard. Finally, we were now at the top of the doctors' priority list.

Robin's diagnoses came back as Malignant Fibrous Histiocytoma (MFH), a rare form of Osteogenic Sarcoma, or bone cancer. After further tests, we learned the tumor had emerged out of her left pelvis, had broken through the integrity of the bone, and had grown rapidly due to the increased levels of estrogen present during pregnancy. In short, Robin had a high-grade tumor, and the likelihood of her survival was a terrifying ten percent.

> *In short, Robin had a high-grade tumor, and the likelihood of her survival was a terrifying ten percent.*

Because she was pregnant, we made all of our decisions mindful of both Robin and the baby. Wanting to make the wisest choices we could, we learned more about MFH, the treatment, the diagnosis, the prognosis, and the chemotherapy needed. We studied the likely results, the chances of survival and everything in between. Throughout it all, we focused all our energy equally on Robin and the baby, and the survival of both precious lives.

The doctors, however, had a very different perspective.

At thirty weeks, the very end of her second trimester, they wanted Robin to terminate the pregnancy so she could undergo aggressive treatment. "If we beat this, you will be able to have other children," they told her. "Without the treatments starting immediately, you will only live for six months."

Robin's sole concern was for our baby. We checked with a neonatologist to discuss our unborn baby's viability. Seventeen years ago, many of today's medical advancements for pregnant women were not available. The doctors told us if we forced the delivery, the baby would suffer from either a low survival rate or very high chance of permanent, life-long disability. Guided by her maternal instincts, Robin knew that every day the baby matured inside of her, the healthier he would be. She also knew that every day she went without treatment, she jeopardized her chances of survival.

Every family makes decisions for important reasons.

For Robin and me, our decisions are deeply rooted in our desire to follow our faith. We focused on the creation and gift of life. Robin never considered terminating the life of our son growing within her. We had two lives to save.

At this point, the tumor confined Robin to bed while on a 24-hour epidural to mask the pain. Looking at her through all of this, I began thinking, *"How did we get here?"* This disease ripped at our family. The tumor dislodged me from my instructor pilot duty, Robin's mother was taking care of our daughter and our son was essentially killing Robin because of his need for a mother's normal, hormonal changes. Because the increased estrogen acted as an accelerant to Robin's tumor, the very biological change giving Jake life was taking it away from my precious wife. Here was my wife of four years, 29 years old. She was bed-ridden with a large tumor on her left backside that caused discomfort when lying on her back, while her pregnancy prevented her from lying on her stomach. She had suffered through ridicule, skepticism, and labeling as a hypochondriac. After enduring Tylenol with Codeine, Percocet, and a morphine pump, she now had a tube injected directly into her spinal cord.

> *Because the increased estrogen acted as an accelerant to Robin's tumor, the very biological change giving Jake life was taking it away from my precious wife.*

Then one unforgettable day, in the midst of all this suffering, Robin leaned over and looked at me as I was kneeling beside her bed and asked me, "Will you raise the children?" A question like this certainly puts everything into immediate perspective.

Without hesitation, I answered, "Yes."

"Then tell the doctors we are going to wait however long it takes until the pediatricians say the baby is healthy enough to be born normally. Only then will we fight this."

On January 20, 1993, after considering the progress of our unborn baby, the pediatricians recommended that we proceed. Robin delivered our son via C-section at 32 weeks. They immediately rushed Jake to the NICU, because the left valve of his heart did not correctly close. While this condition is relatively common with preemies, the added health complications were scary and nerve wracking.

As Robin recovered from undergoing major abdominal surgery, she endured a battery of every available medical test. The one I remember most was the CAT scan directed needle biopsy. After the doctor inserted a large needle into her left pelvic area, the CAT scan took a picture. He then adjusted the needle, and took another picture. As he collected tissue samples, he continued poking and documenting for some time.

A couple of days later, the lead doctor told me he had some good news and some bad news. Following my mother's guidance, I insisted on the good news first, as I sorely and desperately needed good news.

"The tumor fully encompasses your wife's left pelvis bone, which connects to her thigh bone," he stated. "We need to amputate her leg."

"I told you I wanted the good news!" I protested.

"That is the good news," He answered quietly. "The bad news is… she will be dead within six months."

I stood there, numb. How could I possibly respond? Needing some relief, I asked the doctor if he had any guidance to offer.

"Yes," he said, "I recommend we do *not* do the surgery but monitor her pain. For her, it is better if she dies a whole person."

I couldn't believe what I was hearing, and was unwilling to accept this diagnosis as fact. From that moment on, I started looking for a second opinion. With the wonderful help of Robin's sister, Debbie, we found one.

On February 10, 1993, Robin was flown from Colorado to Massachusetts General Hospital, where the orthopedic oncologist removed a volleyball-sized tumor from her left pelvis.

I questioned, "A volleyball?"

"How about a large cantaloupe?" was the answer.

"Well, that's a volleyball."

In the resection process, the doctors removed half of her left pelvis. By grafting part of her sacrum (tailbone) and securing the graft with two bolts, these doctors performed a bone-preservation surgery, which saved her left leg.

Robin lost eight pints of blood in surgery. (After witnessing firsthand the life-saving power of blood donation, to this day I am a regular donor, a tradition now joined by both Sararose and Jake!)

For two days, she recovered with a breathing tube in the Respiratory Intensive Care Unit (RICU). Meanwhile, our little preemie, Jake, remained in Denver, Colorado and faced surgery to correct his heart complications.

Fortunately, after receiving steroid shots, Jake's heart started properly functioning and he escaped surgery on his fragile four-pound-fifteen-ounce body. Once Jake's health stabilized, the Air Force medivaced him to Logan Airport in Boston, Massachusetts, allowing Jake to reunite with his mom on Valentine's Day.

Meanwhile, our little preemie, Jake, remained in Denver, Colorado and faced surgery to correct his heart complications.

The Massachusetts General medical team confirmed Robin had six months to live. For four of those predicted months, Robin remained in the hospital recovering from her C-section and cancer surgery, while beginning an intensive chemotherapy protocol. Because we feared that Robin's life might slip away quickly, we decided to christen Jake while she was still alive. In Robin's hospital bed, my brother baptized Jake.

Her battle with cancer lasted for several years, but Robin proved the doctor's estimated life expectancy wrong. She fought the hair loss and the funny stares. She endured ongoing poking and prodding, tests, shots, x-rays, vomiting (a side effect of chemo), and needles, while she watched some of her cancer-support friends not survive. After treatments, additional surgeries (one of which removed the temporary bolts, because originally the doctors did not expect her to live) and many prayers, Robin beat back cancer.

To this day, both Robin and Jake enjoy life.

Along the way, I realized the financial industry does not offer much guidance on how major diagnosis affects survivors and their legacy.

Because of her battle, the cancer unfortunately sentenced Robin to a life without more natural children. Undaunted to the hopes of a large family and as a way to give back to society and help others, Robin and I are now foster parents. Since 1997, we have fostered twenty-four children, adopting four of them. All of our children are precious gifts and we thank God for each one of them.

Along the way, I realized the financial industry does not offer much guidance on how major diagnosis affects survivors and their legacy.

If you are facing a difficult diagnosis, be assured you can do it. You need to do it. Your family is counting on you. Don't let them down.

I am here to help you from my own experience and I hope this book can help to serve as your financial guiding light.

2

Your Legacy:
More Than Just A Memory

Who are you?

What are you made of? What do you believe? What are your accomplishments, great and small? Whenever you leave this earth, what are you going to leave behind? How are your family and loved ones going to remember you?

These are some tough questions to start off a book about financial planning but, as you move forward with constructing your financial plan, you need to know where you are, who you are, and what you want to leave behind. When you have a good understanding of these questions and your answers, you will start to know what your legacy will be.

Financial planning probably remains low on your priorities right now. Your strongest thoughts may be connecting with your loved ones or it may be focusing on the diagnosis itself and diverting all available energy towards a successful outcome. This is what Robin and I did. We had to make her more than a photo in a scrapbook, so we took videos with her and the children playing together, as she was concerned that the photos were not "alive." We even started

You may not have thought about it, but a major part of your legacy hinges on the memory of how you transition your wealth to your loved ones.

9

taping messages on the tape recorder for the children to play back at certain birthdays, like sixteen, eighteen and twenty-one. As important as other issues appear to you right now, you have to consider your finances and the legacy that you will someday leave behind.

You may not have thought about it, but a major part of your legacy hinges on the memory of how you transition your wealth to your loved ones. Your financial decisions can result in a smooth transition or your decisions can make it a costly and time-consuming mess. Do you know of a relative who had a huge mess when a spouse died? Did the spouse spend countless hours trying to square everything up and find out where all the accounts were? Did he/she know where the safety deposit box key was? Where the will was? Did the person who died even have one?

This guide will help you be the person others will remember for having their act together and everything in place. Remember, how smoothly and uncomplicated your estate transitions will be one of the last memories and statements you make to your loved ones.

As I work with others, every now and again someone will say to my surprise, "Oh, I will be dead anyway, so I am just going to let my heirs fight it out." Unfortunately, fighting is exactly what they will do.

As you consider your legacy and how to transition your assets, take time and reflect on the following questions:

- Who will inherit my assets?
- Who will distribute my assets?
- How are the assets going to be distributed?
- Do I give money outright or flow (schedule) to my heirs over time?
- If payments are going to be scheduled, what are the "triggering" events?
- Who will be the guardian for my minor children?
- Do I want the guardian also to have control over their assets?

- Who will be my caretaker if I need one at the end of life?
- Do I want my heir(s) to have use of the assets but no ownership?
- Who do I want to make decisions for me if I am too sick to make them on my own?

In my personal plan, if my wife and I die while we have minor children in the house, we have designated one person to raise them, another person to manage the estate, and a third person to distribute it. We created this plan because we wanted to relieve those taking care of the children from the burden of tending to money matters and vice versa. Each task contains enough challenges. By separating these responsibilities, we also built in a "checks and balances" for the children's care, if we are not the ones doing the caring.

If you have a large estate, a blended family, perhaps a second marriage, children from the first, Dad remarried after Mom died, or any other complicated dynamic, this book is a must-read: *Best Intentions, Ensuring Your Estate Plan Delivers Both Wealth and Wisdom* by Colleen Barney, Esq., and Victoria Collins, PhD, CFP® (Dearborn Trade Publishing, 2002).

Best Intentions delivers insightful lessons showing how the best of intentions don't always happen and why, more often than one may think, they flat out do not even come close. I encourage you to review the authors' many stories just to see how vital articulating your specific goals become when it relates to transitioning your estate and leaving a legacy.

In *Best Intentions*, Barney and Collins state:

> "We know many clients and friends who focus only on probate avoidance or estate tax reduction when preparing their estate plan. We would like to challenge them and

you to think about what your estate plan says to your family. Does your estate plan pass on wisdom and lessons you would if you were still here?

How can you pass on your estate in a way that insures that you have provided more than just cash to your loved ones?"

They go on and ask three simple questions:

1. If you die today, do you still have important lessons left to teach your loved ones?

2. If you could see what you left behind, what would cause you the greatest disappointment, the greatest pride, and the greatest sense of accomplishment?

3. What unintended message may be sent to your loved ones in your current plan or by lack of a plan?

WOW! These three powerful questions cut through a lot of noise and chatter. They cut through the concerns of probate and taxes. Have you taken the time to write down your wishes? Have you articulated them to anyone? Perhaps it's time to do so.

Family Harmony

As you consider your financial plan, you need to recognize you will leave more than money. Throughout this book, we will talk about mistakes others have made including the misguided belief that money is the only legacy we pass. It always troubles me when I meet with survivors and they say, "I will be gone, so I'll let them worry about it." Without realizing it, this attitude contains danger and, perhaps, some mean-spirit. You must promote family harmony as part of your legacy, your last statement to your world, your family and friends. Don't underestimate your role in your family's harmony.

Write Out Your Wishes in Plain English

When it comes to your estate planning documents, I recommend you write down in plain English what you want your estate to do. How you want it to be distributed and why? Who gets what, and why? If you have a concern about a divorce, this is the place to mention it. To maintain family harmony, one family writes a letter for one of their children. Here's why:

———

"I will be gone, so I'll let them worry about it."

———

> Steven is a delightful ten-year-old son of a friend. With all Steven's wonderful attributes, he struggles mentally with connecting concepts and has difficulty making those concepts fit in the real world.

> His family predicts Steven will become an automobile mechanic. He loves cars. One day he will love to work on them and be pleased someone will actually pay him to do so! If his parents die, Steven will be the only one of their children who will receive his inheritance over his lifetime and will not have any assets given outright to him.

> If all of a sudden he received his entire inheritance at once, one of his "friends" would want to go to Las Vegas and help him spend it! Because it sounds like a great idea, Steven would probably go and enjoy the heck out of himself. However, when he returns to town, Steven won't really understand why his boss has fired him from his job, why his friend has abandoned him, and why he has no money remaining.

> As part of their documentation package, his parents have written him a letter as to why they made this decision and told him they love him dearly and this choice protects him. Without this explanation, perhaps he would not understand why his brothers and sisters all received their money at once and he didn't.

After you put down your thoughts on a plain piece of paper, you can sit down with a qualified estate planning attorney and discuss in plain English the legal documents needed to put your desires in place. You will also have a personal letter expressing your feelings for your family to cherish forever. Additionally, if an heir (or would be heir) challenges the estate, then this letter could be used to further document your true intentions. Sometimes plain English conveys your wishes better than legal jargon! This letter also proves helpful because a will does not always explain *why* you distributed your assets a certain way.

Family Love Letter

Each of us will leave a legacy. Will it be a legacy of confusion or of information?

There is a booklet called *Family Love Letter* which provides one way to help you write out your thoughts. Very few available planning tools have touched me more than the *Family Love Letter*. Donna Pagano, CFP® president of Family Love Letter, LLC, and her team have created a wonderful workbook asking the reader to consider writing down important wishes. This way the family will know what you want them to know, when you are unable to personally tell them.

"While many clients are reluctant to discuss the tragedy of their death or disability with family members, they have less concern about leaving written information behind. This is the purpose of the Family Love Letter. Fundamentally, estate planning is not about the dead and the avoidance of a death tax. Instead, its most important goal should be to provide "A LEGACY FOR THE LIVING."

"Each of us will leave a legacy. Will it be a legacy of confusion or of information? Will we add to the trauma of our death or incapacity by adding to its inherent confusion, or leave a road map to those who follow? Will

14

we leave a *Legacy for the Living*—of the stories, hopes and desires for our family?

The Family Love Letter is a gift—of time, love, clarity. When you or a family member prepares one, you help create a *Legacy for the Living*."

I am so impressed with her workbook that I encourage you to consider ordering one. The web site is www.FamilyLoveLetter.com.

Location of Your Important Papers

I recommend you place a piece of paper in a Ziploc® bag and leave the bag in your refrigerator. On this paper, put directions and locations of all of your important estate planning documents, phone numbers, and such.

Why the refrigerator? If something happens to you, friends and family will come in to care for you. They will eventually go to the refrigerator to see what you have to eat! Moreover, if they have a special diet, they will buy their own food and put it there. Everybody knows the location of the refrigerator. You can't misplace it, and you certainly can't hide it. Therefore, if you store your important documents in there, or at least the directions as to where they are, then no one will have to search to find them. Your family will find your *Family Love Letter* and important papers in a timely manner, and there will be no confusion as to your wishes. One client asked me if the paper gets "freezer burn." I don't think so. In fact, it will be in a temperature controlled, low humidity environment and will never fade.

Be Careful If You Favor One Child Over Another

It concerns me greatly when a client gives preferential treatment to one child over another. Normally the story sounds like this: "My two oldest children are doing well [either through hard work or because of their marriage], but the youngest struggles. You see, the oldest one started his own business [became a doctor, married a doctor] and the second one joined the military [has a steady job, always knows how to make money], but the youngest vacillates in and out of trouble [has been married a couple of times, went to jail for a couple of years]. I am going to leave the youngest a greater share of money because he needs it more."

There may indeed be a valid reason in your case, but your heirs will likely *interpret* an unequal distribution of your assets as an unequal distribution of your *love*.

Also, what does this say to the two successful children? Did you somehow devalue them because of their success? Does their hard work and good fortune mean you loved them less? By giving the third child more money, does it reward the negative behavior? Does it enable this child to continue down a bad path?

> *There may indeed be a valid reason in your case, but your heirs will likely* interpret *an unequal distribution of your assets as an unequal distribution of your* love.

Here's another example:

A family has two sons, Tom and Bill. Tom does well for himself. He put himself through college, became an engineer and makes a good living. He has a stable marriage with three children. Bill is the wayward one. He went to college but didn't graduate. Got married because his girlfriend was pregnant but the marriage didn't last. He works low-paying, manual labor jobs and never seems to earn enough. Bill fell into the wrong crowd and ended up trying to make a fast buck the illegal way. He went to jail for three years and came out none the better. "He isn't a bad kid," his mother would say. "He just makes bad decisions." Every holiday the family would get together. Tom and his family would travel to his mother's home. Bill would always say, "Can't make it this year; don't have the money to get there."

Consequently, Mom would pay his way. Mom always paid his way and never offered anything to Tom.

When their mother died, without explanation, she made an uneven split in favor of Bill.

The issue isn't the amount of money, but it is about Mom's legacy. How did her children interpret the uneven split? What legacy do you think her children inherited? Do you think she facilitated family harmony between her sons? Did she transition her intended legacy? What type of character did she leave her children?

If you intend an uneven split, you may wish to plainly acknowledge your justification. This explanation allows the family to have a clear understanding that this doesn't reflect your love. Acknowledging the reason for the uneven split can often prevent fighting and bad sentiments among family members. This should be one of you legacy goals.

Probate Need Not Be Feared

Probate is the legal process that transitions ownership of the deceased's assets. As simple as this sounds, we all have heard stories about how the courts held up the distribution of assets for years. We have seen the drama spill out of our televisions about some celebrity who didn't have proper estate planning documents and everything ended up in probate. An ensuing battle occurred.

However, we don't hear that the vast majority of estates "sail" through probate with no issue at all and are usually settled in nine months. Probate need not be feared. You do not need be avoid probate like the plague. Probate doesn't suck everything down a dark hole. Yes, probate fees can be high, but usually aren't.

You may wish to avoid probate if you think one of the heirs or someone who believes he/she should be an heir will challenge your estate.

17

Mind you, avoiding probate won't prevent the challenge. If you anticipate creditors will claim assets, if you have a lien on your home or a judgment against you, then you may wish to avoid probate. Nevertheless, it won't prevent the creditors from coming.

One example of a successful probate was with my client Nadia and her mother Jean.

However, we don't hear that the vast majority of estates "sail" through probate with no issue at all and are usually settled in nine months.

Jean just passed away sixteen months ago. She has two adopted children and named the oldest, her daughter Nadia, to be the executrix of her estate. Nadia kept her brother informed of the assets and let him inspect as desired. The estate portion went through the probate process with the help of an attorney. Jean's estate totaled slightly over $2 million. The debts and the taxes were all paid. Official notices were published and trips were made back and forth to the court house. Nadia did most of the legwork, going here and there, while the attorney only performed the essential legal functions and I helped with the financial transactions. There were no challenges, no problems, and everything went smoothly. The total fees were $7,500.

My mother passed away in 2000. She named the oldest of her five sons the executor and everything, except her small IRA, was probated. No problem. No hassle. No challenge. Done. Countless estates go through probate with no problem. If you have prepared well and have titled assets properly (discussed later in more detail), then there should be no problem for you either. Be careful because there can be financial disasters by trying *too* hard to avoid probate.

Samantha passed away in Seattle eighteen months ago. I am working with her daughter Danielle, who has one brother. The will states "share and share evenly." Samantha and her husband purchased the Seattle home fifty years ago and today the home represents her largest asset. The home, originally purchased for $30,000, eclipsed $400,000 at Samantha's death.

When her husband died, Samantha received a step-up of his cost basis as normal. Because she had heard only negatives regarding probate, Samantha changed ownership of the home and added both her

> *Be careful because there can be financial disasters by trying too hard to avoid probate.*

children to the deed. That is the good news. By doing this, she avoided probate and by operation of law, the children became equal owners at her death.

The bad news is by adding the kids to the deed, she *gifted* to them part ownership. Additionally, according to current tax law, if someone gifts an asset while alive, the gift comes with the original cost basis (how much was paid for it in the first place). Without realizing it, she gifted them her *original* cost basis of fifty years ago.

As the children try to sell the property, they face a depressed housing market. The property has not sold yet, but will likely fetch about $350,000. As an alternative to Samantha gifting the home to the children while alive, if the children inherited the home through the probate process, they would be looking at a $50,000 capital loss (date of death value of $400,000 minus the potential sale price of $350,000). Instead of being able to take a capital loss, Danielle and her brother will each pay a hefty capital gain tax based on the original (now gifted) cost basis of fifty years ago!

We figured out this tax represents nearly *eight times* as much as probate would have cost.

As mentioned earlier, you will hear concerns about the probate process. Don't be blinded by all of the negatives.

Note: When one challenges an estate, the judge suspends the probate process until settled. Challenges come from all kinds of places, from family members who think they are owed more than what was given, to last-minute document changes cutting someone out, to creditors who stake a claim against the estate.

Second Marriage

Second marriages possess the potential for very tricky estate planning. You may have children from your second marriage, as well as from your first. How do you treat assets you brought into the marriage? Do you set aside money to your child from the first marriage? How does this decision influence your relationship with your current husband/wife and new children?

> Beth and Rick married right out of college. David was born one year later and when he was two, Rick died at the age of twenty-five from cancer. Luckily, he prepared and purchased adequate life insurance to care for his family. Eight years later at age thirty-two, Beth married Steve. Steve was divorced and has two daughters. Together they have two more children. Beth told me when she mentions David's inherited money, Steve becomes very agitated. Steve complains he pays for all the expenses of the children from his first marriage, the children he and Beth have as well as David, even though David has his own inherited money. Steve is bitter towards David.

As this story unfolds before my eyes, I am uncertain how it will end up. Beth remains adamant about not spending any of David's money, except for David directly, and not for the other children. I fear the relationship will not end well.

If you marry late in life, how are you going to treat the assets? What if your wealth eclipses that of your new husband/wife's? Do you keep your money separate? Do you want your assets available for your husband/wife's use through a trust, in effect delaying the transfer to your children until his/her death? Make sure you discuss these integral concerns about your family dynamics with your financial advisor and attorney. He/she can help you with important ideas and offer wisdom along the way, all the while helping you create your intended legacy.

> *Do you want your assets available for your husband/wife's use through a trust, in effect delaying the transfer to your children until his/her death?*

Your Current Husband/Wife's Authority at Your Death

Many state laws grant strong authority to the surviving spouse at the passing of the other without regard to the length of the marriage or the number of past marriages. You have to be absolutely certain your wishes are clearly spelled out in your estate planning documents. If not, your new husband/wife will decide such things as where you are buried, what the headstone says, the details of the final service, and all other considerations. If no will exists or if the will is not located, the courts will generally defer to him/her over your adult children, and he/she will decide where your heirlooms go. Depending on your state's intestate laws (the laws that govern when there is no will), he/she may have to transfer a certain statutory percentage of your estate to heirs, but he/she doesn't have to transfer your antique tea set or your prized jewelry. He/she can keep the heirlooms for his/her family.

You can avoid significant strife and angst by executing your estate planning documents. These documents spell out your wishes and bypass unneeded confrontations.

You Will Never Be 100 Percent Certain

When creating your will and trust documents, you most likely have a good idea of where and how you want most of your assets to go. Nevertheless, be aware, some issue may be nagging you. Maybe one of your children might be getting divorced or it could be someone in your husband's family has treated you very poorly, causing you to consider making a change. No matter today's issue, there likely will always be an issue. You may never be one hundred percent certain as to where and how your assets transfer.

Too many people delay the whole process because there were one or two issues not settled.

Please don't let this uncertainty prevent you from creating the documents in the first place because you think there will be a better time. Too many people delay the whole process because one or two issues were not settled. Perhaps they were ninety percent certain on all of the other issues, but the smaller ones paralyzed them into doing nothing at all. You can amend documents at any time so go ahead, move forward with creating your documents now, and work on the smaller issues as they develop.

Now Is The Time For Action - Create Your Documents

I hear time and again all the excuses for not getting important estate planning documents in order. You can think of many excuses; perhaps you have said them yourself or you have heard them from others. Almost nothing I can think of should prevent you from moving forward to create your estate documents, especially if you have important information about where you *don't* want your money to go, or if you have minor children. Here is a situation that occurred years ago.

> I did not know Martha, but her family tells me she was lovely. Her family welcomed her death after a long life and short illness. Martha had one daughter and one son. The son had fallen on hard times and suffered financial trouble with an IRS judgment against him. To avoid her money going to the IRS, Martha willed her

entire estate to her daughter, Teresa, who promised to share with her brother "under the table." Sadly, Teresa died instantly in a motor vehicle accident three weeks after Martha. Stephanie is Martha's granddaughter and Teresa's daughter. As Teresa's only child, Stephanie inherited everything from Martha and from Teresa.

At twenty-two, Stephanie maintained a relationship with a much older man (fifty-three). She relied on his help and direction (and you guessed it), had most of the money placed in a joint account with him. After he left (Yep! with the money), her uncle (the one with the IRS problems) sued Stephanie for his share.

Martha could have avoided all of this with proper planning. Don't compromise your legacy because you didn't take the time to establish a plan or create important documents.

Thoughts

It's your legacy. You have the time to set it straight and to help transfer what you truly intend to. You may not have given this much thought but you need to realize that you leave a legacy. When the doctor says it's cancer, or any other life threatening disease, you need to make sure the legacy you are planning to leave is the legacy you *actually* leave. Keep reading this book

> *When the doctor says it's cancer, or any other life threatening disease, you need to make sure the legacy you are planning to leave is the legacy you actually leave.*

and I will help with your financial planning legacy. Now go create yours.

23

3

Estate Documents You Must Have, No Matter What

After choosing your desired legacy, you must create the infrastructure that will actually carry out your wishes. Without important legal documents in place, your desires will not become reality. Every financial plan should include your desired legacy to those you leave behind. You probably know of a family member or a friend who remembers the horror story about probate and how assets didn't transition properly when his/her loved one died. As part of your legacy, you may wish to establish a goal to make your transition as easy and painless as possible for your heirs.

I am very gratified when heirs thank me and say, "Everything was in order. You and Dad did a great job."

As we start your planning, always keep in mind your desired legacy to your family and friends. Your estate documents become your last statement to them. They will remember how the assets transferred.

Let's resolve to get it right.

Overview of The Importance of Estate Planning

You decide where and to whom the assets go. You, not a judge, decide if a charity, church or other entity receives the money.

You prevent the ugly scene of family members fighting over your legacy.

You decide who the guardian for your minor children will be and how to care for your special needs adult child.

You decide to avoid probate or not.

You decide when you die, you transition more than money; you leave behind family harmony and life lessons.

You decide what legacy you leave.

You decide that your last statement to your family and friends is, "I love you."

Planning With Love

Gloria Lenhart learned the hard way to navigate the world of widowhood when her husband passed away. She created a web site you might find useful, www.planetwidow.com. Among other great thoughts, Lenhart discusses "six ways to say, 'I love you.' "

1. Sign an Advance Health Care Directive.
2. Make a list of your assets.
3. Consolidate your accounts.
4. Keep beneficiary forms up to date.
5. Review your life insurance coverage.
6. Update your will and/or trust.

From the list of six steps, there are three essential estate planning documents everyone should have.

1. Health Care Directive, Advance Directive, Living Will
2. Last Will and Testament
3. Durable Power of Attorney

(We will discuss the need for and applicability of Trusts later in Chapter 4, *Trusts*.)

Health Care Directive, Advance Medical Directive, Living Will

Although all estate planning documents are important, the Advance Medical Directive probably just became the most important. When faced with an end of life diagnosis, you have to consider the fact that you might lose control. Your body has just let you down. You can either go along for the ride, or you can take control of your treatments. The diagnosis compels you to learn about the treatments, the side effects and the potential outcomes. It also forces you to consider what qualities of life you most cherish. Now you must consider when you may decline treatment, but most importantly, it encourages you to take control.

Your body has just let you down. You can either go along for the ride, or you can take control of your treatments.

One sure way to take control is by signing an Advance Medical Directive. Depending on the state where you live, the document outlining your wishes for medical care is called a Health Care Directive, Advance Directive or Living Will. Although not directly a financial document, the Health Care Directive becomes critical to securing your legacy. This important document expresses your wishes as to the medical treatment to your body if you are unable to make these decisions yourself. Sadly, this was Terri Schiavo's situation. For reasons the public was not aware of, Terri lived in a vegetative state. Her husband said she would not want to live like this. On the other hand, her parents said she was responding and they would care for her. The problem was no one knew what *Terri* wanted.

What level of care do you want? Do you want extraordinary measures to intervene to keep you alive? Do you want a feeding tube, breathing machine, or other medical care? How do you want your religious beliefs honored? Whom do you want making these decisions for you?

How about your vital organs? Have you considered anatomical gifting, or the gifting of your body for scientific research or study? Depending on your diagnosis, this might not be possible, but you may want to look into the options you have.

Unless you properly express your important wishes in writing, they will not be known by others and a judge may have to step in.

The health care directive remains dormant while you are capable of making decisions for yourself and only comes into power when you are unable to do so.

Because of your diagnosis, you may need to prepare for the use of this document. My mother died of lung cancer in a hospice, but they had on file her health care wishes and knew she did not want any heroic intervention. They also knew her status as a DNR (do not resuscitate) patient.

You may wish to update your documents to reflect your faith and the directives your faith dictates. You may also wish to include language reflecting your religious views.

Although not directly a financial document, the health care directive becomes critical to securing your legacy.

Take the following measures:

> 1. Consider your wishes regarding medical treatment and end of life decisions. Incorporate your religious beliefs and wishes and share them with your doctor and family.
>
> *Note*: Many religions have sample language and sample documents on their web sites. You may wish to review your religion's information for appropriate language and direction.
>
> 2. Based on your wishes above, execute the appropriate documents needed in your particular state.
>
> *Note*: If you might receive end of life care in another state, make absolute certain you have that state's recognized language in your documents. Not all states recognize all other states' documents.
>
> 3. Execute as many original documents as needed. Give one to your attorney-in-fact, one to the medical staff, one to your place of worship, and have one for your records.

4. Discuss with your doctor your decision and see what specific documents the medical facility where you will receive care requires. Some hospitals prefer their own documents for liability and protection reasons.

5. Discuss with your family these documents and let them know what you have decided. Keep these documents available to them and not locked away where they may not be found or be unable to be unlocked for whatever reason.

6. As your health condition changes, review these documents and make appropriate modifications.

Note: There will be an expense to create these documents. Do your homework on the costs and pay them. The expense to make an amendment should be much lower than the original cost of creating the document in the first place. Either way, pay the fee. I know what I am saying here may seem insensitive, but you don't have the time to pinch pennies or complain about the cost of preparing these documents. The heartache and angst avoided by having the documents in place will more than pay for themselves.

Your Last Will and Testament

Your last will and testament contain your last words to your family, friends, and heirs. This legal document outlines your intentions on how to settle your estate. In the will, you direct assets to family, children, grandchildren, and others. You may include a friend or those who have touched you in some meaningful way. You may even specifically eliminate someone.

The will carries no authority while alive and only becomes legally unchangeable at your inability to make independent decisions, normally at or near your death. The will defines the transition of your assets, but your legacy lives long after the division of the estate.

Personal Representative, Executor or Executrix

In the will, you have the ability to nominate your Personal Representative, Executor (if a man), or Executrix (if a woman) who will settle your estate. Whether this person is called *personal representative* or *executor(rix)* depends on the state you live in. No matter the name, your representative's function and responsibility are the same.

You will need to give consideration as to whom you nominate. If your husband/wife is alive, you will likely nominate him/her to be your personal representative. If he/she is not alive, then many will generally nominate the oldest child. Give consideration as to whether the oldest child's personality and life experience best suits him/her for the role. Sometimes the best suited one lives closest to you or has a business sense on how to settle financial matters, and not necessarily the oldest.

Maybe your personal representative shouldn't be a relative at all. Many people will automatically name their husband/wife to be their personal representative. This customary and traditional decision might not be the best one, especially now, in a moment of great stress and uncertainty. You should base the importance of choosing your personal representative on this person's character and values, rather than on "blood." Within any decisions, many gray areas exist when settling estates. Consider the fact that your personal representative can make decisions completely *against* your wishes but well within the law and the guidelines set forth in your will.

Consider the fact that your personal representative can make decisions completely against *your wishes but well within the law and the guidelines set forth in your will.*

Below is an example of such a situation within the law, but certainly not what Connie intended.

> I never met Connie, but I did meet her son George. Connie had two boys, George and Pete. Connie's estate nearly topped $900,000, including the home and a stock

portfolio of $400,000. As George was the oldest son, Connie named him executor. As their dad had already died, the will said each son receives half: nothing fancy and pretty straightforward.

Through the normal probate delays, the time to divide the property came about a year after Connie had passed. George and I worked up the date of death value on the stocks, and he said he would get back to me as to which ones went to Pete and which ones he would keep.

I thought this was odd. Normally, I have seen where there were ten stocks, the number of *shares of each stock* would be divided by two and each would receive those ten stocks with half of the shares. This certainly would be what his mom wished when she said split everything 50/50. George did not do this.

George knew the value of her portfolio at the date of her death was about $400,000. He tracked their progress one year later. He gave Pete all of the *underperforming* stocks and kept the better performing ones for himself. One year later, the value of the portfolio was about $440,000. Pete received about $180,000 because his stocks had actually lost money from the time of his mother's death, and George received $260,000 because his share had performed better.

George honored the will by splitting the account 50/50 using the date of death value, not the value at the time of the split.

Some will say Pete has the ability to sue his brother, but think of the expense and the disruption. I am not suggesting George get away with it, but instead, I use it as an example of why naming a third party, non-family member might the best choice to accomplish your wishes.

A delicate balance exists when you determine who your personal representative should be. You want someone familiar with the family, but perhaps not part of the family. You also want someone completely objective, but who won't operate independently without considering family wishes. However, being able to blame no-win situations on a non–family member may have strong merit in keeping family harmony long after the settling of your estate.

> Laura had three daughters who were close to each other and to her. When Laura passed away from congestive heart failure, she had named her oldest daughter as her personal representative. Everything proceeded smoothly with the estate settlement until the decision of a certain piece of artwork in Laura's bedroom. The painting became a significant flash point with two of the daughters, the oldest and the youngest. Each had very valid reasons for wanting the painting, and each set her heart on getting it. The painting had some monetary value, but the reason for wanting it was the emotional connection to their mom.
>
> Because the value of the painting tilted the amounts, the oldest daughter reshuffled other assets to her youngest sister to make the inheritance "even" in dollars. However, price wasn't the issue.
>
> Unfortunately, you can see what happened. As the personal representative, the oldest sister decided to keep the painting for herself. She now displays it proudly in her home. The youngest sister for a while refused to set foot in the home and missed important family celebrations.

This seemingly simple decision turned into a potential destroyer of the sisters' relationship, family harmony and their mom's legacy.

Caution: The decisions your personal representative makes will have a legacy effect *attached* to you. If there had been a separate non–family member settling the estate, then Laura's daughters would have understood the painting couldn't be ripped in half and only one of them could actually inherit it. Also they would have had someone other than the oldest sister to blame.

Guardian

Certainly all parents with minor children, especially single parents, must have a will. This document names a guardian for them. One of the hardest decisions you make will be choosing the guardian for your minor children.

The decisions your personal representative makes will have a legacy effect attached *to you.*

How do you consider one side of the family over the other? Sometimes you have a clear choice, but many times it is not. Do you name the one who has no children, or the one who already has a couple of children? Do you name the most successful one, or the one who struggles a little to get by?

In our will, we have given Robin's sister the ability to make capital improvements on her current home to accommodate our six children. Certainly, she will need to add a couple of bedrooms and bathrooms to care for their basic needs. We have authorized her to use part of *their* inheritance to do this. We have spelled out other provisions so if something happens to us; Robin's sister will have little or no financial disruption.

Note: You need to name a guardian for your child the instant you become pregnant. If you do not nominate the guardian and something happens to the parents, then a court will decide. Even if the court gets it right, there will be many hurt feelings along the way as one side shows how they are "better" than the other and how the other side just isn't fit to be parents. No need for this. Having no will would be a terrible legacy to leave your family and your children.

Remember you may also wish to name someone other than the guardian as the manager of the children's inheritance. You may have nominated the guardian because of her love for children and her willingness to do so, but she may not have the ability or inclination to handle the money. You may recall my personal estate design nominates three people: the guardian, who is different from the estate manager, who is different from the person who authorizes payments. These checks and balances assure everyone's interests remain pure.

There will never be anyone as good as you and your husband/wife in raising and caring for your children. As such, there may always be doubt. Your selection of guardian may never be 100 percent perfect, but don't hesitate naming someone who is as close as possible.

You may want to take the time to write a letter to your children letting them know of your wishes for them to do certain things. Perhaps you want them to take clarinet lessons (as Robin did) or play soccer (as I did). You may want them to attend a certain high school or college or pursue a certain major and course of study. I would want the children to grow up in my faith, so this would be included in the letter. I would caution you not to make this letter overreaching so if the child doesn't get into the school you wanted, they don't feel like they let down their deceased parent. Be supportive of them with insights from you. You can make this letter part of your will.

There will never be anyone as good as you and your husband/wife in raising and caring for your children.

Review your will often. Relationships change, people move, family members get divorced. The naming of a guardian is critical and should not be a "make-it-and-forget-it" decision. As life events change, you may wish to nominate a more suitable guardian based on updated information.

Durable Power of Attorney

Just like the health care directive grants authority over your person (your body), the Durable Power of Attorney grants authority over your assets.

General Powers

You have the ability to grant power to someone "to become you" for decisions, financial and otherwise. Your agent can have the power to sell your property, open accounts in your name, enter into binding contracts (binding you), and perform all matters you can. Be careful as to whom you give this general power. If you don't put limits on it, the person you grant the power to can act on your behalf at any time.

You have the ability to grant power to someone "to become you" for decisions financial and otherwise.

Strategy: Consider creating this document and giving the power to family members or even neighbors *without* giving them the actual document, just yet. The granting of powers does not require that they have the document for use right now. However, if in the hospital recovering from an illness or accident, you could then direct them to the location of the document and have them operate on your behalf (without having to worry about the power being misused).

Limited Powers
You can give limited powers to perform very narrow functions or to perform broader ones. For example, you can give very limited authority to your neighbor to sell your home. Let's say for some reason, you move out of the local area and your home still has not yet sold. You give your neighbor limited power to sell your house. (I did this when Robin was going through her cancer treatments in Massachusetts and I needed to sell our home in Colorado.)

You can also give limited power to perform for a certain period of time until a certain date or event and then the power expires. For example, while on a world tour vacation, you can grant a limited power until you return.

Springing Powers
Springing power comes into being only at certain predetermined events. Let's say you create a springing power that will take effect if hospitalized. This power remains dormant until/unless you are admitted into the hospital. You could give springing power for any measurable event and then end this power until another measurable event. For example, you could give power if recovering from a surgery and end this power when discharged from the hospital.

Powers of attorney have great flexibility but can lead to great misuse. Be careful whom you give this power to.

Note: No matter which kind you have, you can only execute a durable power while you have the ability to make independent decisions. All powers end at your death.

Note: The person you have granted power to has no ownership in your assets; he/she just has the ability to function on your behalf.

One Other Important Consideration
Beyond the essential planning with your three documents discussed above, you may wish to consider planning funeral arrangements.

Funeral Arrangements
I remember very clearly when I was a young teenager admonishing my mother, "Mom, you really should stop smoking."

"Honey," she said lovingly, "I have been smoking for twenty years now, ever since I was sixteen. I don't think I will ever stop smoking."

With my immature view on life, I retorted, "Sure, Mom, one day you will stop smoking." Indeed, after smoking for forty-two years, she died when she was just fifty-eight years young.

The doctors diagnosed mom with lung cancer at fifty-six. At this point in her life, she had been smoking at least two packs of cigarettes daily since sixteen. The doctor pronounced she would have about eighteen months to live. The year was 1998. Robin enjoyed being a five-year survivor having completed all of her treatments and now my mom was going to start her chemotherapy and radiation.

Through the process, Mom maintained her strong faith (the faith she passed to her five children). Mom started to plan her funeral service and worked with my oldest brother finalizing all of the details. Together, they decided on the songs, the readings and other liturgical issues.

She also went to the cemetery and purchased her grave site along with her head stone. Accomplishing this ahead of time gave her the ability to work with the cemetery officials and select her final resting place. Mom selected the plot closest to the water pond. A large tree nearby "will give me shade during the hot Louisiana summers," she would say. I do not know for certain, but I would not be surprised in the least if she spent some reflective time there.

She did a complete financial review and beneficiary check. Other details were completed. She purchased the casket and selected the pallbearers. Mom even selected her favorite picture for the official notification and the funeral program. Everything, I mean *everything*, was in place to the last detail: everything except for the date.

Contrast this pre-planning with perhaps someone you might know. Do you know of a friend or relative who did no planning? Then the family had to make decisions in haste. Perhaps the children had competing thoughts about songs, pallbearers, etc. What could be worse? What if you *had* planned but no one knew and only afterwards your family discovered your wishes?

I have already made known to my family certain songs I would like sung at my funeral as well as some of the pallbearers. This may seem morbid, but after Robin's earlier diagnosis, my mother's preparations and the fact Robin's mom passed away due to inflammatory breast cancer, I know death is part of my life and want to be prepared for my family's sake.

> *Everything, I* mean everything, *was in place to the last detail:* everything except for the date.

Thoughts

Your legacy and documents need to be coordinated or your wishes will most likely not become reality.

Your estate planning documents and the way you have titled your accounts (see Chapter 5) becomes one of the most important components of your plan while alive and at death. You can work hard at earning money, creating wealth through investments, safeguarding against bad decisions, but all for naught if you don't have estate planning documents in place.

You need to write down end of life decisions and your preferences in such a way the state recognizes your wishes. If you don't have them, create your documents today. If you created them years ago, please see your professional team and determine the current validity of your documents based on today's laws and if they will indeed transition your assets and your legacy the way you intend.

―――――

You can work hard at earning money, creating wealth through investments, safeguarding against bad decisions, but all for naught if you don't have estate planning documents in place.

―――――

4

Trusts: Clearing Away The Mystery

There seems to be some strange aura that enters the discussion at the mention of the word trust, referring to a document that you might need. Trust. The first thought that comes to mind with the word trust centers on a reliance about whether I can count on a person for honest and accurate information. However, when used as a legal document, many will report they have no idea what constitutes a trust. After reading this chapter, you will understand the definition of a trust much better. Trust me.

A trust is a legal document established within current laws to help you control your assets while alive and direct them upon your passing. Significant legal considerations and other contingencies exist when creating trusts and other documents, therefore it pays to seek legal advice concerning these documents.

I presume there will always be clients confused about trusts, even those who have established them. I will share with you an analogy to help you visualize how and why a trust works. Trusts, used correctly, can be wonderful planning tools.

Note: Don't let the technical terms prevent you from planning. We will discuss them in an easy to understand manner.

Trust

In your mind, take out a large keepsake box and open it up. Put it on the kitchen table, the night stand or the coffee table right next to where you are reading this. A trust is like your keepsake box. As simple as it sounds, you can put items in the box, and you can take them out. You can put in a checkbook, a deed to property, car keys, and stock certificates, and you can always remove them.

Just like on the outside of a Campbell's® soup can, you will see instructions, recipes, and ingredients. The keepsake box also has a set of instructions, recipes, and ingredients directing the transfer of the money. Whatever the grantor (the person who puts assets into the box) directs, the transfer will flow accordingly.

While alive, the grantor can put in and take out whatever he/she wants to. However, at the grantor's incapacity, due to death or illness, the successor trustee will then shut and lock box. Once locked, only the instructions on the outside of your keepsake box control the assets inside the box (titled into the trust). Like the soup can, the ingredients labeled on the outside will instruct the successor trustee as to how to handle the assets on the inside.

Like the soup can, the ingredients labeled on the outside will instruct the successor trustee as to how to handle the assets on the inside.

The grantor can create an unlimited number of provisions and directions for the trust. Generally, the grantor directs under what circumstances to release the estate and to whom. The trust, therefore, *directs and flows* the estate to those who will inherit it.

Statute allows for many different types of trusts. There can be charitable trusts, special needs trusts, or revocable living trusts, just to name a few.

Remember, the lawyer creates the trust; you define your objectives for the trust and move assets into the trust (with the help of your financial advisor).

Note: You can create more than one trust. As such, you will need to identify *which* trust controls and distributes *what* assets. Titling the assets in the name of the trust you want them in moves them into that trust. If you don't title them into the trust, the trust will not govern them.

Some Definitions

Grantor: the person who puts money into the trust. Normally you are the grantor, and you have the trust titled in your name.

Trustee: the person(s), or organization who has the authority over how to manage the assets inside of the trust, within the guidelines (instructions, recipes and ingredients) of the trust itself. Normally with revocable living trusts, the grantor and the trustee are the same person.

Titling: Most trusts are titled like this:

> The Shak Hill Trust
> Shak Hill, Trustee
> U/A 7/17/2007 (U/A stands for Under Agreement and
> the date reflects the trust creation day.)

Note: You will see variations on the titling of trusts. The name has no material meaning, but generally gives a clue as to the purpose of the trust. For example, the title might be The Hill Children's Education Trust, then you would have a clue the money would be for the Hill children's education. (The title does not have to give a clue. The grantor could name it Trust No. 1.) As no universal standard exists, essentially, you choose the name within certain common guidelines.

Successor trustee: A will has a personal representative or executor(rix); a trust has a successor trustee. The successor trustee is the person or entity (like a bank trust department) who will succeed the original trustee when he/she either resigns or becomes unable to serve.

Co-trustees and co-successor trustees: The grantor can name co-trustees and co-successor trustees to serve. The grantor needs to be certain whether he intends for the "co's" to work together or separately. If together, this arrangement can be very burdensome, particularly if one of the co's lives out of the area. If he requires both to work together, then both signatures are needed on every transaction, no matter how small. This requirement might mean overnight mail and the possibly of it being lost, not to mention coordinating between work schedules, vacations, and illnesses. Although designating co-trustees sounds like a great idea, in practical terms it might not be. If you are concerned about one trustee taking advantage or having favoritism over another, then he may wish to name an independent trust department where they will operate without prejudice.

> *Although designating co-trustees sounds like a great idea, in practical terms, it might not be.*

Beneficiary: The person, people, or organization(s) named to receive assets.

Purpose of Trusts

The very versatile trust has many different uses. An individual creates a trust within certain legal guidelines making each trust uniquely different in accordance with that individual's objectives. As a rule, individuals use trusts for similar purposes discussed here.

Directs Your Money

The number one purpose of a trust is to "flow" your money according to your wishes. The trust lets you stagger the disbursement of money over time or give it out all at once. It lets you set thresholds of achievement, either naturally at certain ages or after certain accomplishments. You can put parameters on the distribution (flow) of the money to the beneficiaries based on whether or not certain events or objectives are accomplished.

Let's review some examples for flowing assets to beneficiaries, but know the list of possibilities is unlimited.

- Once twenty-one, then they inherit "x" amount ...
- At age thirty they receive "y" amount ...
- After graduating from college ...
- Once married ...
- After the birth of their first child ...
- After graduating from graduate school ...
- If not in jail ...
- If not dependent on illegal substances ...
- As long as no criminal record exists...
- If they join the military ...
- If they receive an honorable discharge ...

You have nearly complete control as to when, how, and under what conditions you flow the money. You can set benchmarks as described here based on accomplishments or distribute the money merely based on age. You can restrict the flow to a beneficiary with a history of irresponsible behavior or criminal activity. By delaying ownership of the assets when using the trust, you can allow the recipient(s) time to mature and become more responsible as they accomplish certain tasks and obtain certain ages.

As you can see, the choices are endless. If you want to *restrict* the flow of money, you cannot do so under a will, and thus the trust becomes the only document available to do so.

> Barbara's net worth hovers around $1,350,000 including her home. She has two sons; one is responsible. He is married and has Barbara's only three grandchildren. The other son has never been married and has been in jail for minor offenses twice. Barbara wants the first son to have his portion of the inheritance at once without restriction on her death. However, she wants the second son to clean up his act. She has directed the successor trustee to

release some of the money if he earns his college degree, if he holds a white-collar job for over a year, and if he stays clean for five years.

Barbara needs a trust because she wants to flow the money under certain circumstances to her second son. She can name the responsible son, her bank, or anyone else she chooses to be the successor trustee. A will alone does not work in this case.

Additionally, if you have special-needs children, you can schedule an income stream and not let the child have access to the principal. You can start with an income stream, change to a lump sum, and return back to the income stream. Only your imagination limits the possibilities when it comes to trusts.

Takes Advantage of the Applicable Exclusion and Tax Planning

The second reason for a trust comes with the ability to take advantage of your applicable exclusion allowable under federal law. The applicable exclusion allows you to shelter a certain amount of your net worth upon your death, free from federal estate tax, to your heirs. The value of your estate above this exclusion amount will have a death tax consequence.

Note: If single, then you *automatically* get the exclusion amount and having a trust does not help you bypass estate taxes. In the year 2009, the exclusion amount is $3.5 million. In 2010 the tax goes away and enjoys a one year repeal. Hold on, don't be too ecstatic; because of the sunset provision, the old law comes back in 2011 and the exclusion resets back to $1 million. The federal tax treatment of estate is an ongoing debate in Congress and the laws may change in the next few years.

(More about this important consideration is discussed below on page 50, Applicable Exclusion.)

Avoids Probate

Avoiding probate constitutes the third most important advantage of the trust.

Every citizen in the United States is first a citizen of a state. States create probate laws. Although similarities exist, each state has its own legally defined method in which to process or transition their citizens' assets. The probate process has associated expenses, takes time to wind through legal requirements and will delay the transfer of assets to those who will eventually end up with them.

By using a trust, you have outlined with a legally recognizable document your wishes of how your estate will transition. Because you have taken this step, the assets named into the trust will bypass the probate process and go directly to the named beneficiaries.

Avoids Estate Challenges

The fourth benefit comes if someone challenges your estate with a lawsuit. The instructions and wishes of a trust are often viewed to be harder to challenge than those of a will. For example, if you created or amended your will very near death, then there could be a challenge as to whether you properly executed the will, if you were of sound mind, if someone exerted undue pressure, or if coercion of any kind occurred. In contrast, if the trust has been in place over the last six months or six years and has been operating normally, the court may deem a trust a truer representation of the wishes of the grantor.

_____

The instructions and wishes of a trust are often viewed to be harder to challenge than those of a will.

_____

Don't let me mislead you here. I have spoken with many attorneys who repeatedly tell me they make a good living based on the lawsuits arising from contested trusts. The existence of a trust doesn't mean there won't be a challenge. It just means the courts won't have to probate the asset, which has *absolutely nothing* to do with a challenge or not.

Protects Privacy

Privacy becomes the fifth reason for a trust. The will becomes a public document for all to see. The trust remains private. Many say privacy is a good thing; after all, why is it other people's business? On the other hand, with little oversight, no one watches the successor trustee to ensure the wishes are being carried out as desired. Unfortunately, the successor trustee may not always act in the best interest of the deceased, but in his/her own best interest. With everything, you will have to weigh the pros and cons.

Privacy can also be a detriment if the grantor of the trust becomes incapacitated and the successor trustee has a stake in the remaining assets at the grantor's death.

Alice created a trust and named Jen, one of her two daughters, the successor trustee. When Alice became ill and unable to handle the trust, Jen stepped in to become the successor trustee making financial decisions for Alice's trust. Alice also named Jen her Health Care Directive agent.

Unfortunately, the successor trustee may not always act in the best interest of the deceased, but in his/her own best interest.

Because Jen is one of the beneficiaries, she will have a very real conflict of interest. Does she spend top dollar for Alice's care and risk depleting funds she would receive at Alice's death? Jen might think, "Mom will die soon anyway; she doesn't even realize I am here."

A sad and unfortunate possibility exists when quality care can be restricted so there would be more money to transition. Because the trust names the other daughter as a beneficiary, she will have the ability to know what is going on, but other family or the public will not.

Funding the Trust

Many times at the creation of the estate plan and again at the first death of either the husband or the wife, you will need to re-title your assets into the trust accounts. You will need to divide the estate into the several accounts per the trust instructions. Make sure you work with your professionals to help you develop and implement your planning strategy.

Most likely, you will be working with your financial advisor to help you with this part of the plan. The best financial advisors will coordinate with your attorney, insurance agent, and accountant to implement their recommendations in your plan.

The best way to illustrate this funding step is with an actual case.

> Robyn and Bob were married for twenty-five years. Both had been married before and both of their spouses had passed away, leaving them each with two children. When they married at age forty-seven and forty-five, they knew they would not have children together, but they wanted to care for each other while alive and leave their part of the estate to their respective children. In 1995, Bob and Robyn established trusts deciding what should happen when the first of them died. In 2000, Bob passed away. I met Robyn in 2005, and all of the assets were in her single name. She did not title any of her assets into the trust. Robyn had not funded the estate plan as directed in the estate documents.

Even those with trusts seem to miss the concept of "funding" the trust. To help, I have come up with a simple, yet powerful analogy. I tell my clients the lawyer builds the house (the trust) and my job as the financial advisor is to move in the furniture (fund the trust). If the furniture remains on the sidewalk in front of the house, the furniture will not be within the control or protection of the house. Similarly, if the account remains in single name (or name other than the trust) and is not titled into the trust, it will be outside the control of the trust document.

If the furniture remains on the sidewalk in front of the house, the furniture will not be within the control or protection of the house.

Because Robyn had not titled assets into the trust, the trust would not govern them. Her will would control the estate, which was destined for probate. Even though she had a well thought out plan with top-quality trust documents, because she titled everything in her single name, those trust documents would have been useless. Her will directed all her assets split evenly between her two children. Because the combined estate surpassed $3 million in net worth, if she died in 2011, her exclusion amount would be $1 million, leaving the remaining $2 million taxable to her heirs. At the 45% estate tax bracket, her estate would be subject to approximately $900,000 in taxes. Additionally, her two children would inherit everything and leave Bob's children with nothing. Most likely, Bob's children would file suit against her children for their part of their father's estate.

> Robyn showed me the estate documents. They directed at the first one's death, the survivor to create three separate trusts. The estate would be valued and divided in half. Because Bob directed his assets into his trust, he maintained an estate and used his applicable credit when he died. At his death, his trust received the exclusion amount allowable based on the year of his death. The second trust received the rest of his half of the estate. The documents then directed Robyn to place her entire half of the estate into her third trust.

> By actually funding the estate plan (moving in the furniture) the way she and Bob decided, we were able to save the estate over $350,000 in taxes, create an income from both of Bob's trusts to Robyn, and prevent any potential lawsuit.

Robyn has moved to Florida where she needs to establish domicile. I also advised her to restate her trust and other legal documents as "Legal resident of the State of Florida." Her documents created in Virginia need to become consistent with Florida law. Quite a mess was diverted.

By actually funding the estate plan (moving in the furniture) the way she and Bob decided, we were able to save the estate over $350,000 in taxes...

Other Considerations

As mentioned previously, the trust has many different uses and is a very versatile legal document. We've addressed the purpose of trusts, now let's look at some other considerations.

Pour-over Will

If you have decided you want a trust to distribute all of your assets, you will want to have a 'pour-over' will.

At your passing, each item you own either will transfer by operation of law or will settle to your estate and be probated (see page 64, How Assets Transition To Heirs). When all of your assets are accounted for, those assets governed by your estate, and hence your will, could be "poured over" into a trust after the probate process concludes. By having a "pour-over" provision, you ensure your trust will eventually distribute any assets not specifically titled into the trust as if they were in the trust in the first place.

You would *not* want a pour-over will if you want assets to go in multiple directions. For example, if you have two or more trusts, each transferring assets in different directions, then you don't want a pour-over will. You would have taken particular care to title assets into their specific trusts. Additionally, if you wanted only certain assets to transition via the trust, and the rest of the assets to transition via the estate, you would not want a pour-over provision.

Here is an example for the use of a pour-over will:

Mildred loved both children equally. She created a trust giving all of her assets equally at death to her children outright and immediately. To make sure she didn't miss anything, she created a pour-over will to redirect all of her assets to her trust. This way, if there was an account she forgot about, or if she had assets unable to be titled (like jewelry or art), then they would all be governed by the trust because the estate was poured-over into it.

Here is a case when it might not be as useful.

Gloria belonged to many organizations, many for pleasure and some for philanthropic reasons. As a board member of several charities, she planned to leave a substantial amount of money to each of them. As with many families, Gloria has concerns about some of her heirs and wants to set up different distributions for her children and grandchildren. She created three trusts: one for the children, another for the grandchildren and the third for her charities. Gloria does not want to have a pour-over will as her assets are going in more than one direction (because she has three trusts). She has taken great care to title all of her assets into one of the three trusts, creating separate brokerage accounts, changing the beneficiaries on her life insurance and her IRA. If she acquires a new asset not titled into one of the trusts or if she overlooked something in her planning, she may not want to automatically pour-over this asset.

Ownership versus Use

An important consideration regarding transitioning assets to your heirs is whether you want them to have ownership of the assets or if ownership stays with the trust. Consider the differences particularly if you think there will be a creditor, predator or divorce situation with your heirs.

If your beneficiary receives the asset outright, not only does he/she have use of the asset, but he/she has ownership and all of the associated liabilities. If a trust holds the assets and the beneficiary never receives them at all, your beneficiary will have *use* of the asset, but won't have *ownership* (and won't have the associated liability as well).

Consider your car. When you die, you decide to give this car outright to your oldest son, Joe. Joe now has both the use and ownership of this car. If this car gets

> *If your beneficiary receives the asset outright, not only does he/she have use of the asset, but he/she has ownership and all of the associated liabilities.*

into an accident, there will likely be a lawsuit for damages. If found liable, the judgment can reach "through the car" into Joe's personal possessions for damages, even if Joe wasn't driving! What if the damage award of millions of dollars? The judgment would extend to Joe as the owner, and could attach his personal assets to pay for the damages. With ownership comes direct liability.

> *Joe would then have access to the car, he would have the car keys, but he would have no ownership.*

Instead, what if you gave the car to your trust? You could allow the trustee to provide Joe a lifetime use of the car. Joe would then have access to the car, he would have the car keys, but he would have no ownership. Therefore, if he gets into an accident, the lawsuit would not involve Joe as he is not the owner. None of Joe's assets would be subject to the judgment.

If we take this example to the extreme, let's say you put all of your assets into trust for Joe's health, education, maintenance and support. Let's further say Joe has no assets of his own. He owns nothing. Not the car, not the house, not the gold watch. Because you directed, he has *use* of these items, but no *ownership*. Well, if Joe has a creditor, a predator, or is subject to divorce, Joe would have no assets to pay a judgment. How could he pay if he has no assets of his own to pay the judgment? Trusts have strong protection against the actions of the beneficiary. Statute affords incredible protection to the trust (or keepsake box) against lawsuits.

High-end estate planners will recommend this technique. You may wish to look into it for your family.

Spendthrift Clause
A spendthrift clause provides additional protection. In general, this clause prevents excessive amounts of money to be withdrawn without the permission of the trustee.

If there is a tendency to overspend, the beneficiary might just blow the inheritance. This clause allows the trustee to deny excessive withdrawals from the inherited trust assets and acts as a safeguard protecting the beneficiary from him/herself.

If the beneficiary has a judgment against him/her for damages, this clause will also protect against the excessive withdrawal, as the trustee is unlikely to authorize such a payment.

Taxes

Many clients think just because they have a trust means they won't be paying any taxes. Not true. Under the tax code, income tax is never forgiven, so even if your total estate rests below the estate tax threshold, money representing income, such as retirement plans and the gains in annuities, will *always* incur income tax considerations. In addition, those who have wealth in excess of the applicable exclusion threshold will still have to pay associated taxes. Consider Bill Gates. Just because he has created trusts (which I can only presume), this doesn't mean he skips paying estate taxes. The trusts will flow the money, the number one reason for trusts in the first place, but they won't avoid the tax after using the applicable exclusion.

With the spendthrift clause, the trustee can safeguard the beneficiary from creditors, predators and divorce (and him/herself).

Complex estates routinely use trusts in their planning. A number of trusts shelter assets from current taxes. Some trusts can generate income for you with the remaining principal going to charity at your death. Other trusts transition your personal residence to your heirs while you're alive in a tax-efficient manner. Others will help transition assets if the surviving spouse is not a U.S. citizen. Still other trusts are used for special-needs children. Taxes are complicated and I am not a tax professional so please consult a well-qualified attorney to discuss these important strategies.

We have discussed trusts and the functions they provide. Trusts provide meaningful advantages, but be aware, like anything else, you may get sold a trust even if you don't necessarily need one. Many people have bought a trust they really don't need. Just make certain you need one before you pay for one.

Applicable Exclusion

As discussed above, every American has the ability to leave his or her heirs a certain amount of assets estate tax-free. The deduction amount called the "applicable exclusion" represents the greatest deduction the federal government allows its citizens to have.

Note: This book does not consider the merits of an estate tax, just notes that one exists and that tax law makes the applicable exclusion available.

The applicable exclusion amount has changed over the years. If one's total estate value falls under this exclusion, then the estate pays no estate tax. If over, the amount of your estate exceeding the exclusion would be subject to federal estate taxes. Current law repeals the federal estate tax in 2010. You may remember years ago when Congress passed and the president signed the "repeal" of the estate tax. Well, like many things in Congress, this was just smoke and mirrors to some degree. The estate tax does go away in 2010 and the old law comes back in 2011, bringing back the old estate tax.

Current law repeals the federal estate tax in 2010.

Let me explain using a train track analogy. Picture a train track straight and true. For miles, it continues to go straight down the line. This straight track represents the old estate tax law. Congress created a new law which detoured your estate train away from this track. The law forced all the trains on a detour from the year 2002 through 2010. This detour turns and twists its way through increasing applicable exclusion amounts (see table) to eventually reconnect with the original straight and true track when the old law comes back in 2011.

For example, if your husband died in 2004, then his allowable exclusion amount was $1,500,000. Hopefully, this amount was sheltered within his trust.

Look at the table.

Applicable Exclusion*

2002–2003	$1,000,000
2004–2005	$1,500,000
2006–2008	$2,000,000
2009	$3,500,000
2010	estate tax repealed but the gift tax remains
2011 (back to old 2001 law)	$1,000,000

* http://www.irs.gov/pub/irs-pdf/p950.pdf (page 5)

Many think Congress will work on clarifying this estate tax issue. With the current climate in Washington, some believe they will just let the law expire, bringing back the old law and the much smaller exclusions. Stay tuned. This will become an important issue very soon.

UPDATE: As of this writing, Congress has passed no new bills. However, strong belief anticipates that the Congress will pass and the president will sign a permanent solution to the current unknown estate tax law mess. Many believe they will lock in the 2009 rate of $3,500,000. This will mean that the repeal in 2010 and the re-set to the old law in 2011 will most likely not occur.

Cheerios® Coupon

Many clients come to me confused about the applicable exclusion. They want to know how to take full advantage of it. Here is the best analogy to help illustrate the point.

Think of a box of Cheerios®. At checkout, the cashier more than willingly charges you full price. On the other hand, if you use a $.50 off coupon, he/she is more than willingly takes $.50 off the purchase price.

You have to use the exclusion amount before it expires and you have to use it correctly.

If you forget to use the coupon, it has expired, or the coupon is for Cheerios® when your purchase is for Frosted Flakes®, then he/she won't accept it. Additionally, when you get back home and you see the coupon on the kitchen table and return to the store, it will be too late to use it (without going through much hassle).

Well, the applicable exclusion is similar to the Cheerios® coupon. You have to use the exclusion amount before it expires and you have to use it correctly. The primary method of using your coupon comes through a trust.

Note: Each citizen has the right to use his/her credit so if married, both of you will want to use your "coupon." Because you don't know which one of you will die first, you both will need to have a trust.

Married Couples

Many husbands and wives have the typical "I Love You" wills. This means at the death of the first, the survivor will inherit everything. Without a trust, a keepsake box, to capture the applicable exclusion, the one who dies first transfers all of his/her assets to the survivor. As such, the deceased forfeits his/her applicable exclusion.

The survivor inherits all of the assets estate tax free due to the unlimited marital deduction. The unlimited marital deduction grants tax relief to the inheriting citizen spouse and does not trigger a current tax due. The law *delays* the tax until the death of the surviving spouse. As attractive as this may sound, if the estate is over $1 million, this becomes a bad planning technique.

In contrast to the "I Love You" plan, if the married couple uses trusts, then at the first death, the trust will hold those assets titled into it. This proper technique eliminates taxes up to the applicable exclusion. The survivor does not inherit this part of the estate. With planning, the survivor would have use of the money as well as some access to the trust assets. Typically, the trust provides for the survivor's use, so those assets remain available to the survivor.

The best way to explain is with an example.

> James and Sue have been married for twenty-six years. James owns a small technology company and they have a combined net worth of $1.7 million. The life insurance

policy in James' name has a death benefit of $1 million. As it appears to be the case, the "Bush tax cuts" will expire (officially the tax cuts will "sunset") and the old estate law will come back. If this happens, the applicable exclusion will be re-set to $1 million. The doctors have just diagnosed James with leukemia. They each have an "I love you" will leaving to the other all of their individual estate.

If James dies in year 2012, his assets go to Sue. She inherits everything from him leaving no estate remaining in his own name. Because he did not create a keepsake box, a trust, to hold his applicable credit, he loses his ability to shelter any estate. Sue, now with an estate of $2.7 million ($1.7 million plus the life insurance of $1 million), receives his assets estate tax free, thanks to the unlimited marital deduction. This estate planning technique serves merely to delay the taxes, now due at Sue's death. This technique does not eliminate the tax. If Sue dies without any new law changes, her estate will automatically shelter her applicable credit of $1 million. The additional $1.7 million will be subject to federal estate taxes, and at a potential rate of 45%, the estate will have to pay nearly $765,000 in tax. (The tax would be even higher presuming the estate grows in value, which is likely over time.)

Strategy: James and Sue both create a keepsake box, a trust. They title assets into their separate trusts. Even though James is diagnosed, we still don't know he will be the first to die. Stranger things have happened. Presuming James does die first, then his estate will fund the trust to the maximum allowed under the applicable exclusion, which in our example is $1 million. His trust would be available for Sue to use while alive, but could be isolated to grow over time with proper investments. Then,

55

when Sue dies, her trust shelters her applicable credit, $1 million, leaving $700,000 exposed to taxes. The tax rate with an estate of $700,000 is lower so for our example, let's use 37%. The estate would owe $259,000 in estate taxes. Compared to the tax with only an "I Love You" will, with a trust vs without, the trust generates a savings of $506,000! In addition, what is even better, James' trust can grow to any amount (with proper investments) and the entire trust will pass to his heirs completely tax-free. (While his trust grows, current income taxes are due, but at the death of Sue, the principle that remains transfers tax-free. Please see your accountant for a complete discussion on tax issues.)

Compared to the tax with only an "I Love You" will, the trust generates a savings of $506,000!

Citizenship

If married, citizenship matters. When the surviving spouse is not a US citizen, the unlimited marital deduction, enjoyed by married citizens, does not apply. Without getting into all of the details, evidence suggests surviving non-US citizens eventually return to their mother country after the death of their citizen husband/wife. As a consequence, non-citizen spouses do not enjoy the ability to delay the taxes through the unlimited marital deduction provision enjoyed by citizens. As the citizen spouse would normally remain in the United States with all of the estate assets, the unlimited marital deduction serves as merely a delay in the estate tax, not an elimination of it. As the non-citizen likely returns to the mother country with the inherited estate assets, the estate tax becomes due immediately after the death, which could greatly affect the lifestyle of the survivor, whether the non-citizen actually stays in this country or not.

The reason the taxes are immediately due is because the federal government does not want untaxed assets to leave the country without first being taxed. Just like the Cheerios® coupon discussed earlier, a proper planning technique is available, but has to be correctly implemented.

By creating a specific kind of trust called a Qualified Domestic Trust (QDOT), the non-citizen survivor can delay the taxes and prevent the immediate depletion of the estate due to the estate tax.

Essentially, the QDOT will hold the assets of the deceased citizen. The trustee has to be a US citizen and becomes liable for the proper payment of taxes as the trust distributes assets to the surviving spouse.

As the IRS is a potential loser here, be sure to use a well qualified attorney to create this trust for your family if there is a non-citizen husband/wife.

As a consequence, non-citizen spouses do not enjoy the ability to delay the taxes through the unlimited marital deduction provision enjoyed by citizens.

Post Death Planning

Not all is lost if a death occurs before the final documents are signed. Important post-death techniques may be beneficial to you and your family. The window for such decisions narrows quickly. Working with a lawyer in a very timely manner can allow for some post-death estate planning, but with this course of action, many mistakes can occur and opportunities may disappear because of seemingly small, yet technical issues.

Important Note: Each state has its own rules and laws governing trusts and post death planning. Please use this information as an educational guide and not specific to any state. You should work with a competent estate planning attorney to coordinate your situation to the laws of the state you live in.

Thoughts

Just because you have taken the time and the expense to set up a trust doesn't mean you are finished. You need to fund the trust. As I said earlier, the best analogy I use is simple to explain.

> The attorney builds the house; your job (and your financial advisor's job) is to move in the furniture.

Remember, you have to re-title all of the assets you want into the trust. The checking account, savings, brokerage, money market, and car as well as beneficiary changes to the 401(k), IRA, and annuity contracts all need to be re-titled into the trust (that is, if you want them to be governed by the trust).

Note: Check with your attorney as to the wisdom of titling your personal residence into the trust. Some states, such as Florida, give strong protection to homeowners; therefore, it might not be in your favor to title your home in the trust. Virginia, where I live, does not grant strong protection, so placing my home in a trust might have advantages.

Both your estate planning documents combined with the titling of your assets need to complement each other. Without coordination, a misapplication will greatly disrupt your estate plan. Your documents may say one thing, but the title and the beneficiary designation may say something totally different.

5

Where are Your Assets and Who Owns Them?

Your illness diverts you and your family down a road where you do not want to be. Nonetheless, it is the road you currently find yourself on. You have to take a comprehensive look at everything you own. The time is now to pull everything out and account for it. You may have been holding some assets or accounts stashed away waiting for an opportunity to use them for a new boat, family vacation, special getaway or rainy day fund. Well, your advisors need to know about it. They also need to know the physical location of these assets as well as your estate planning documents.

Personal Financial Statement

Take all of the account statements you receive and start categorizing them on one sheet of paper. Put cash and CDs in one category, investments, 401(k)s and other retirement accounts in another, and finish with real property. This can be anything from real estate to cars, boats, airplanes to paintings or other material possessions. Add your life insurance and make sure you list the slush account you might have been hiding for a rainy day, or those stamps up in the attic you collected when you were young (like I did). List the safety deposit box, with contents, and identify where the property deeds are.

You will want to account for business interests as well. List all your business ventures, identify your role in them, and who else is involved. While doing this important step, attach a realistic value to these holdings.

Next, look at all of your liabilities. What do you owe, and to whom do you owe it? Place all of these after the asset section. List them all, whether a credit card, bank loan, student loan, bank obligation, etc.

Take your time and be exactly correct. Your assets do not automatically transfer so no matter what, this accounting will need to be accomplished. *Someone* will have to do this first tedious step. You are the best to accomplish this, as you know where all the assets are.

For example, the World War II generation commonly hid assets. Recent stories surfaced about money found inside of the walls of a home as the current owner begins to remodel, or the finding of something buried in the back yard where the swimming pool is about to go. These stories are about someone from the past who had stashed treasures away. Certainly, they didn't do it for those who found it. They did it for their use, or the use by their family. Unfortunately, these buried treasures remained hidden and may be forever lost to the intended family.

Don't let this happen to you and your loved ones. Dust off your treasure map and dig for the hidden money only you know about.

> Someone *will have to do this first tedious step. You are the best to accomplish this, as you know where all the assets are.*

You will find in the Charts and Tables section a worksheet you and your family can use to start the process. Don't underestimate the importance of this step creating your personal financial statement.

As you create you personal financial statement, also indicate on your sheet how the asset is titled. This is a critical step to making sure your legacy wishes are carried out.

Let me ask you the following question:

Why Is Ownership Designation Important?

You need to determine exactly what you own and to what degree you own it. You also need to decide who you want to inherit what and in what form of ownership they will receive the property.

Important Question

Why is the title of the asset critical?

Answer: Because the title will determine which estate document controls the asset and which heir inherits it.

Who Owns Them and How Are They Titled?

Without thinking about it, we own all of the assets that we have. From the informal ownership of our personal goods, like jewelry, TV sets, furniture, and clothes, to the formal ownership of the title of the home, car, checking accounts, and brokerage accounts, we own these assets and at our death, our survivors will become their new owners.

> *In my years of financial planning, one of the most overlooked aspects of owning assets is how they are titled.*

In my years of financial planning, one of the most overlooked aspects of owning assets is how they are titled. When you go to the bank, you often don't give any thought to the banker's question, "How would you like to title the account?" No matter how much thought you put into the answer, how you answer this seemingly innocuous question has significant impact as to how, at incapacitation or death, your account will be handled.

Here are the common ways we own assets and how they will pass when one of the owners dies. Pay particular attention to this as you may want to revisit your ownership options after you have a better understanding as to how they will transfer to your beneficiaries.

Joint Title

The most common title used among married couples is Joint Tenants with Rights of Survivorship (JTWROS). Anyone can use this method of titling, such as a parent and child, business partners, or friends. As the title suggests, joint ownership means both owners have an unlimited right to withdraw the money. The survivor will receive the money at the time the other owner dies. JTWROS ownership bypasses the probate process and by operation of law, this asset becomes immediately available to the surviving joint owner regardless of the value. Neither the will nor the trust govern JTWROS assets.

> Joan, a widowed mother of three daughters, had an estate worth approximately $900,000, of which $600,000 was liquid (in other words, in a variety of cash or near cash holdings such as CDs, money markets, savings and checking accounts). The balance of her estate was in the value of her house, car, and some jewelry.
>
> To avoid living in a nursing home, Joan moved in with the daughter who lived nearby. Her other two daughters lived across the country. Out of convenience, Joan titled all her banking assets so the daughter she lived with could easily effect any changes, renew the CDs, and write checks. Therefore, $600,000 was in joint accounts (JTWROS).
>
> Joan's will said to divide her estate equally in thirds among her three daughters. After she died, however, by operation of law, all the joint assets immediately went to the daughter whose name was joint on the accounts. The personal representative sold the house, car, and jewelry, generating $300,000 in cash, which she put into an estate account. As the will governs the estate account, each daughter received her third, $100,000. So one daughter received $700,000 ($600,000 of joint assets now solely in her name plus one third of the estate) and the other two received $100,000 each. Joan did not intend this unequal distribution.

The situation could have easily been avoided if (1) Joan had given the one daughter Durable Power of Attorney to help with the bank accounts or

(2) Joan had placed on her accounts a Transfer on Death (TOD) to her three daughters, which would have bypassed probate, or (3) Joan had placed her liquid assets in a Revocable Living Trust and named her three daughters as equal beneficiaries. The trust would have bypassed probate as well. Any one of the three options would have protected Joan's wishes and her legacy.

Tenancy in Common

Two or more people use this titling when each owner owns a proportionate share of the account value. The owners need not be related. Because each owns his/her own share, each person has the right to sell his/her share, give it away, or will it upon his/her death. Each owner's will governs their portion of the account.

Tenancy by the Entirety

This account ownership is only available to married couples. Neither owner can dispose of his or her half while alive without the permission of the other. Upon the death of the first, then the other becomes the sole owner. The will and trust do not govern this account.

Single Name

As the name suggests, accounts in single name are yours only. As these accounts become part of the estate, only the will governs single accounts.

TOD/POD

The Transfer on Death (TOD) designation will transfer your account after your death to the named beneficiary. While alive, the named beneficiary has no access to the money. Furthermore, you are not required to even notify the beneficiary that he or

Perhaps a better way to proceed is to give the son a Durable Power of Attorney over this account and have the account titled TOD to the son.

she is even named. At the passing of the owner, this account will transfer directly to the named beneficiary. In some states, this designation carries the title POD (Payable on Death). This title performs the same function. TOD accounts are available on most deposit, brokerage, and other accounts dealing with money. Neither the will nor the trust control TOD/POD accounts.

Caution: Many times I have seen with the death of the first parent, the mom or dad will jointly put his/her only child on accounts because, "he is going to get it anyway." So they now have a joint account. Well, if the son gets into any trouble at all—divorce, lawsuit, or IRS trouble, for example—then this joint asset becomes attachable as an asset of the son, while you are alive. Perhaps a better way to proceed is to give the son a Durable Power of Attorney over this account and have the account titled TOD to the son. With the TOD, if the son experiences any trouble, he doesn't own the asset; therefore, it cannot be attached. At the parent's passing, the TOD will transfer directly to him and bypass probate.

How Assets Transition to Heirs

> *Your assets will not automatically transfer to your heirs or beneficiaries.*

Your assets will not *automatically* transfer to your heirs or beneficiaries. Generally, they will transfer as you have expressed in your will, but state law grants some protection for family members. For example, in many states, the husband cannot completely disinherited the wife in favor of the "lover" or "girlfriend" no matter what the estate document says.

Outside of those statutory requirements, you control how smoothly (or not) your assets transition.

Many factors come into play including different state laws. Do you or did you live in a community property state? Did you acquire assets you still own in a community property state? Do you have assets (like vacation homes) in several states? What assets did you bring into the marriage? The way these assets are titled will have a major impact as to how they transition to your heirs.

64

Presuming you have an uncomplicated estate, let's spend a moment talking about how your assets will transition to your heirs.

Trapeze Flyers

Do you remember the Ringling Brothers and Barnum & Bailey Circus? The one I remember had three rings on the circus floor where performers would display their acts. One of the crowd favorites continues to be the flying trapeze show. During the show, one of the trapeze flyers on the left side of the stage swings out while the one on the right side would time his swing to catch the other. With twists, flips, and death-defying jumps, the show came alive and was quite exciting to see. If one of the stunts missed, then the performer would fall and be caught by the net. Even the "fall" ended up being theatrical at some level.

With the trapeze in mind, imagine that when someone dies all of their assets start falling down the middle of the center ring toward the net. For assets with a named beneficiary, like a life insurance policy, IRAs or 401(k)s, the trapeze flyers will swing out and grab those assets and give them to the named beneficiary. If the account has a TOD designation, then the flyer will swing out and grab that TOD account. Same thing will happen to the joint accounts. For assets named into the trust, the flyer will swing out there and grab trust assets and put them in the keepsake box. (See discussion on *Trust* in Chapter 3 to understand my use of the keepsake box.)

Eventually, the flying trapeze performers will grab all of the assets designated to go somewhere. The remaining assets will fall to the net. In this example, the net is the will. All of the other assets transferred to named beneficiaries *before* they hit the net. The will governs only assets actually hitting the net.

For assets with a named beneficiary, like a life insurance policy, IRAs or 401(k)s, the trapeze flyers will swing out and grab those assets and give them to the named beneficiary.

65

Caution: Many clients think the will governs all of their assets: Not true. The will only governs the assets it catches. The will cannot direct assets you no longer own. Others think they don't have to worry about anything if they have created a trust: Not true. The trust only governs those assets titled into the trust and therefore owned by it. All other assets fall to the net where the will governs and controls their distribution.

> *Many clients think the will governs all of their assets. Not true.*

I have found remarkable success using this simple analogy. People come up to me and say, "Now I get it." Send me an email and let me know if this example works for you.

Beneficiary Check

Because many of your assets can pass outside of probate and will transfer per the title or the beneficiary listed on the contract, you will want to perform a thorough beneficiary check. Every now and again, I hear a story about someone who died and the ex-wife/ husband or ex-girl/boyfriend was still the beneficiary. Good news, some states have statutory protection for the current wife/husband to avoid such a situation. Nevertheless, recovery of the assets requires legal action, expenses and a whole lot of headaches.

Naming Minor Children Beneficiaries

When determining who your beneficiaries are going to be, you will want to give strong consideration before you name your minor children. In fact, I would strongly recommend you do *not* name them. Why? If you do, they will inherit all the money at once. Because they are minors, the court will name a guardian on their behalf. Yes, this guardianship defaults to their living parent in most cases, but what if the parent is not the best suited to manage the children's money.

The court requires significant oversight of this money along with annual updates. Then, when the children reach the age of majority, usually eighteen, the money is all theirs, to spend, as they desire. Probably not the desired legacy of the one who died. Here's an example.

Steve was a track star in college just shy of the Olympic team. He still ran every day and entered many charity marathon events, often winning and then donating the winnings back to the same charity. The doctors diagnosed him with pancreatic cancer. Steve died within months. He had the "I Love You" will giving all of his assets to his wife Sally. Unfortunately, he named their two minor children, who are eight and ten, as equal beneficiaries on his life insurance worth seven hundred thousand dollars. She petitioned (at her personal expense) and because she was their mother, the judge appointed Sally guardian for this money. She now has to make annual accountings of the children's assets through her lawyer (more expenses).

Regrettably, with hundreds of thousands of dollars trapped, she faces either selling their home (in a terrible housing market) or going back to work to generate needed income.

It is unfortunate because Sally's access to this money is very limited and the bank makes it equally difficult for her to withdraw this money, even if used for the children's benefit. In reality, she essentially has little or no access to this money and has to rely on other resources for the family's combined care. Regrettably, with hundreds of thousands of dollars trapped, she faces either selling their home (in a terrible housing market) or going back to work to generate needed income. When the children reach eighteen, they will receive their inheritance at once and in full. Sally told me that she tries to forgive him for what he has done to the family. Steve did not want this result to be part of his legacy.

You might be better served to name your spouse as beneficiary or, if not desired, then at least name a trust benefiting the children. You can then name your spouse as trustee, or someone else. This way you can then schedule the release of this money over time at certain life milestones, such as marriage, birth of children, graduation from college, etc.

Naming One Person to Distribute to Others

Be additionally careful if you name one person as beneficiary with the desire to have him/her care for another or to have him/her eventually distribute your assets to others. Money does unusual things to people's memories and promises. Intentions rarely become reality. I run across parents who name one child as beneficiary to all the money anticipating he/she will distribute it to his/her siblings. This approach is very flawed and you should avoid it.

What if the receiving person has outstanding debts or a judgment against him/her? This money could become attached to settle the judgment. Even if it all goes well, there could be other issues or tax implications when it comes time to give the money to siblings.

> By the direction of the will, Mary received nearly $500,000 from her mother with oral instructions to split the money evenly with her two siblings, a brother and sister. Mom thought this would be easiest as Mary was the most responsible one of the three. Mom gave Mary sole ownership of this money. Once Mary received it, Mom's will would no longer govern the disposition of this money. Mary was free to do whatever she wanted with it. She was no longer legally required to honor Mom's wishes.

Even if Mary wanted to divide by three, she would then need to gift the money to her brother and sister. Each of the children would end up with $166,700. Unfortunately, Mary can only gift $13,000 annually without triggering a gift tax consequence. This will either cause an unnecessary tax, use of Mary's lifetime gifting amount, or cause a substantial delay for her siblings to receive their inheritance.

Thoughts

You need to review all of your assets, where they are and how they are titled. Start with a personal financial statement and list all assets (even those stashed away). Don't underestimate how critical titling is. Also, make sure that the titling matches your wishes and discuss possible pitfalls for each one. The way your assets flow, or don't flow, will greatly affect your legacy.

This will either cause an unnecessary tax, use of Mary's lifetime gifting amount, or cause a substantial delay for her siblings to receive their inheritance.

6

Understanding Your Investment Risk

After identifying where your assets are and how they are titled, the next part of our discussion evolves to the need to understand investment risk. Do not overlook your need to take some risk and the value of it. Conversely, don't take too much risk. Become a *planner* instead of a *gambler*.

Too many times I hear, "I can't afford to take risk right now. I can't afford to lose any money because we don't know what the future looks like." I understand this comment and why people say it, but my concern is, You can't afford *not* to take *some* risk.

The risk you take should not be the "close your eyes and just pick a stock" risk. How crazy would that be? However, you can take an appropriate amount of risk only after you account for emergency cash and known extras. (We will talk more about this in the next chapter.)

Yes, bringing your money to the bank and buying CDs feels very comfortable. Although comfortable, a financial disaster may be heading your way. Buying just short-term, non-growth CDs, for example, is not part of a well thought out long-term plan. You need to invest some of your money in growth opportunities. Your goal may have shifted from becoming the richest couple alive, to just staying even and not going backwards. Understanding your risk will help you get there without a crazy risk roller coaster ride.

Included here is a Risk Analysis Questionnaire, which you may wish to take and score.

Here's how it works:

> Questions one through five measure your attitude toward risk and your willingness to accept risk. Question six measures your years until you expect to spend the money. Remember, *beginning* an income stream is different from cashing out and taking the proceeds to buy something. According to current law, you have to start withdrawing from your IRA at age seventy-and-a-half, but you might not have any plans to cash totally out. For example, if now age sixty-five, you would *not* say you have five years to go. In reality, you would have the rest of your life, hopefully greater than twenty years!

By understanding your risk tolerance, you can, with the help of a financial planner, better prepare a comprehensive plan to work within your risk level, to help you maintain your lifestyle and outpace inflation.

Over the years, I have seen many risk tolerance charts and have created one for my clients.

Remember: Your personal risk tolerance is different from the risk associated with individual stocks and investments. This questionnaire is intended to measure your individual risk and does not reflect the risk inherent with any investments.

The following questionnaire will help you to assess your risk profile.

———

Become a planner *instead of a* gambler.

———

71

Risk Analysis Questionnaire

1. We will risk some safety in an attempt to stay ahead of inflation.

Agree	4 points	
Somewhat Agree	3 points	
Somewhat Disagree	2 points	
Disagree	1 point	score _____

2. We will risk some safety for potentially higher returns.

Agree	4 points	
Somewhat Agree	3 points	
Somewhat Disagree	2 points	
Disagree	1 point	score _____

3. We know the market can go down; we are willing to accept some periods of negative returns.

Agree	4 points	
Somewhat Agree	3 points	
Somewhat Disagree	2 points	
Disagree	1 point	score _____

4. We will accept fluctuating returns in order to potentially achieve our goal.

Agree	4 points	
Somewhat Agree	3 points	
Somewhat Disagree	2 points	
Disagree	1 point	score _____

5. We will accept greater volatility to potentially achieve greater returns.

Agree	4 points	
Somewhat Agree	3 points	
Somewhat Disagree	2 points	
Disagree	1 point	score _____

Now add up the score for your total points and place the number here:

Total Risk Score _____

6. In approximately how many years do you expect to cash out and spend all of this money currently invested?

3 years	1 point
5 years	2 points
10 years	3 points
15 years	4 points
20 years	5 points
Greater than 20 years	6 points

Put your score here for your Time Horizon:

Time Horizon _____

Now score yourself on the chart to identify your potential allocation.

Time Horizon

Risk Score	1	2	3	4	5	6
5	Conservative	Conservative	Conservative	Conservative	Conservative	Conservative
6	Conservative	Conservative	Conservative	Conservative	Conservative	Conservative
7	Conservative	Conservative	Conservative	Mod Conserv	Mod Conserv	Mod Conserv
8	Conservative	Conservative	Mod Conserv	Mod Conserv	Mod Conserv	Mod Conserv
9	Conservative	Conservative	Mod Conserv	Mod Conserv	Mod Conserv	Mod Conserv
10	Conservative	Mod Conserv	Mod Conserv	Mod Conserv	Moderate	Moderate
11	Conservative	Mod Conserv	Mod Conserv	Mod Conserv	Moderate	Moderate
12	Mod Conserv	Mod Conserv	Moderate	Moderate	Moderate	Moderate
13	Mod Conserv	Mod Conserv	Moderate	Moderate	Moderate	Mod Aggressive
14	Mod Conserv	Mod Conserv	Moderate	Moderate	Moderate	Mod Aggressive
15	Mod Conserv	Mod Conserv	Moderate	Mod Aggressive	Mod Aggressive	Mod Aggressive
16	Mod Conserv	Mod Conserv	Mod Aggressive	Mod Aggressive	Mod Aggressive	Mod Aggressive
17	Mod Conserv	Mod Conserv	Mod Aggressive	Mod Aggressive	Mod Aggressive	Aggressive
18	Mod Conserv	Moderate	Mod Aggressive	Aggressive	Aggressive	Aggressive
19	Mod Conserv	Moderate	Mod Aggressive	Aggressive	Aggressive	Aggressive
20	Mod Conserv	Moderate	Mod Aggressive	Aggressive	Aggressive	Aggressive

Stock / Bond

20/80	Conservative
40/60	Mod Conserv (Moderate Conservative)
50/50	Moderate
60/40	Mod Aggressive (Moderate Aggressive)
80/20	Aggressive

74

First, take the time horizon score and circle the appropriate number across the top. Then, take the total risk score and circle it along the left side. Find the corresponding box for your potential risk allocation.

This broad risk score could act as the basis of starting to create your plan. By looking at the previous page, if you scored 'conservative,' you may wish to consider a 20% stock and an 80% bond portfolio. You can see other potential outcomes to your score.

Reminder: This stock to bond mix only represents the *investable portion* of your portfolio and does not include your emergency cash or known extras, which remain separate.

Thoughts

Certainly, in recent years, we have all been reevaluating our investments and by extension, our risk tolerance. Many people make decisions based on short-term emotions and not sticking with their longer-term plan. Short-term emotions will not help to accomplish long-term planning.

Adverse conditions in the financial markets cause some people to let everything ride while others want everything out of the market until things settle down. Resist both of these extremes.

Adverse conditions in the financial markets cause some people to let everything ride while others want everything out of the market until things settle down. Resist both of these extremes. Yes, you will need to reevaluate your risk and the risk level of your family. Use the chart above to help identify where you fall on the risk scale. Use the Wayshak Pyramid® (discussed in the next chapter) to identify your emergency cash and known extras allowing for necessary longer-term planning. Together, this approach will help you identify and fund your short-term requirements and help you identify your longer-term plans.

7

Wayshak Pyramid®:
Important Planning Method for Life

It may seem premature, or even morbid, to think about your legacy as you continue to lead a full life. However, the way you lead you life determines, to some degree, how others will remember you and the nature of the legacy you leave. This chapter shows you a method to create your financial plan during your life. By using this method (or adhering to the one you already have), you will help solidify that part of your legacy associated with your money and your investments, both for today, and for the future.

Over the course of my professional career, clients have looked for some method to combine their investment knowledge with a comprehensive way to create a plan. I created the Wayshak Pyramid® for just this purpose.

As you review your plan, you need to consider the following simple, yet powerful, questions:

1. What are your legacy goals?
2. What financial plan is required going forward in life?
   This question includes two components:
   (a) How much money do you need to keep in emergency cash in order to feel comfortable and sleep well at night?
   (b) What are your known extra expenses between now and the next four years or so?

What Are Your Legacy Goals?

In setting and fulfilling your legacy goals, it is necessary to plan your future life. Paint a color picture of how your life, including retirement, will look. You may want to break your picture into two views: Now and Later. You may have always had a desire to travel, spend time with extended family, or sail the world in your dream sailboat. The best way for you to live is to keep your hopes and dreams alive. What are they? Spend some time writing them down and forecasting what you want to do. You will want to prioritize and start planning to live. What are you going to do first, in the next couple of months, and the next couple of years?

Do you know what the difference between a goal and a dream is? Napoleon Hill (no relation) answered in the following simple yet profound way:

A goal is a dream with a deadline.

Review your list of goals and dreams and put an "accomplish by" date beside each entry. Separate the Now dreams from the Later ones.

Most goals should be practical, but some can be "stretch" goals. Consider even the most outrageous goal, one you would love to accomplish. Even if you feel you don't have the ability to accomplish it, put it down. This "stretch" goal will help you move forward with the rest.

How Much Emergency Cash Do You Need in Order to Feel Comfortable?

As you start creating your new financial plan, the first task starts with determining the amount of emergency cash you need to feel comfortable.

Some experts in the field suggest you have cash to cover at least three to nine months of living expenses. While a great place to start, you must also now consider unknown and unplanned medical expenses. As you have entered this unknown, consider overloading emergency cash until you get a strong handle on the expenses needed for treatment versus how much insurance will cover.

Colon cancer has spread throughout Mike's body. He and Cathy have decided to go to another country to try an experimental drug not yet approved by our FDA. Travel, lodging, time off work and treatment costs are off the charts. If they didn't have the money readily available, they would have needed to liquidate assets, surely at exactly the wrong time, and they could have incurred penalties or fees. By reviewing their plan, they were able to establish the amount of emergency cash normally needed and then *doubled* it for the unknown.

Because of the real potential for unknown expenses right now, you will want to increase your emergency cash account. Do this by changing your dividends to "pay to cash" and stop reinvesting. Consider temporarily lowering your 401(k) contributions to increase your take home pay. You may also want to lower any monthly expenses to the minimum amount and discontinue overpayments.

Emergency cash should be very liquid and easily available.

Emergency cash should be very liquid and readily available. An interest-paying money market represents a perfect place to keep your emergency cash. No, you won't earn a lot of interest on this money, but it will be available without penalty if and when needed. If your emergency happens or not, work with your advisor to adjust the amount you need. Keeping too much money here will be a drag on your well thought-out financial plan.

What Are Your Known Extra Expenses Between Now and the Next Four Years or So?

Once you've determined how much emergency cash you need to keep available, the next consideration is:

> *"In the next four years or so, what expenses do you know are coming up?"*

78

This question does not refer to day-to-day expenses such as your grocery, electric, or mortgage payments. You know about those and they are generally covered with cash flow. I am talking about your other known extra expenses you have coming up over the next four or so years.

For example, are you going to now buy that boat that you have always wanted to buy? How about a plane? A new car? Is there a child starting college or a wedding coming up? What are your normal vacation plans? Does your home need a new roof?

As you identify these expenses, write them down by category and place a reasonable dollar amount beside them. Be fair with the price to avoid under or over budgeting.

How are you going to pay for these known extras? If you have strong cash flow, you may be able to pay for these extras from your current income. On the other hand, the rainy day fund you have accumulated over time might need to be sold and turned into this new goal. Today might just be that rainy day. You have permission to go ahead and sell. If already retired, you may need to reserve this money in anticipation of the expenses coming up.

Let me give you a fun example:

> Ethel came to me at age seventy-two and had no financial plan. She was a retired widowed and cannot generate extra money from her cash flow. After creating a plan with her, we set aside her emergency cash. She told me one of her dreams was when she turns seventy-five, she wants to take her whole family on a seven-night cruise to celebrate this birthday milestone. What a great dream! (In reality, a great goal because it has a built-in deadline.)
>
> The first question I asked her was if she would be willing to adopt me to be a part of her family. She laughed and said no. I then asked how many passengers and how much

79

per passenger. "Seventeen passengers," she pronounced, including a couple of brothers and sisters, her children and their spouses, and all her grandchildren. The price per passenger, she said, was $3,000.

17 passengers at $3,000 per passenger = $51,000 total

The only prudent thing we could do with this $51,000 known extra expense coming up was buy a two-and-a-half-year CD. When Ethel reaches seventy-four-and-a-half, this CD will mature. She's going to go on her seven-night cruise.

Note: She thinks I'm a hero! You see, she purchased this CD in year 2000 when the markets were still heading straight up and other advisors suggested she put this money in a mutual fund so she could grow the money. Every investment should match your goal. Ethel needed funds at a certain date in the future and needed to invest accordingly to make certain her funds would then be available. If she violated the principle of investing short-term money into long-term products, such as a mutual fund, then recent events tell us a mutual fund decision would have negatively impacted her plan. She would have had to leave some of her family on the shore, or cut the trip from seven nights to maybe three.

You have *your* goals and dreams written down. Pinpoint the amount of emergency cash needed to keep you comfortable and able to sleep at night. Then, identify the amount of known extras coming up. With these two numbers written down, you can now move forward and create your long-term financial plan.

Let's Put Some Numbers Down

Considering the concepts of emergency cash and known extras, we can start putting some numbers down. The best way to illustrate the creation of a plan is to talk to you about Mary.

> Mary's husband Bob had a major heart attack eight months ago and finds himself on the heart transplant list. At sixty-one and eligible, Bob retired because of this diagnosis. Checkups are progressing well. After discussions, they determined their emergency cash need is $40,000.
>
> We then looked at their known extra expenses from now through the next four or so years. Mary said she would like a new car; they wanted to do some traveling; the house would need a new roof; and she wanted to give some money to a grandson for college. We also accounted for potentially unknown medical related expenses. We wrote the numbers down and their list looked like this:

New car	$30,000 (in about eighteen months)
Traveling	$16,000 ($4,000 a year for four years)
New roof	$17,000 (in three years)
Grandson's college	$ 5,000 (in six months)
Potential medical	$50,000
Total of Known Extras	$118,000

81

After considering their assets, the 401(k), the stock account, CD's and their cash available, they had $500,000. From here, let's do the math.

	$500,000	available
-	$ 40,000	emergency cash needed to sleep well at night
-	$118,000	known expenses placed in short-term investments
	$342,000	available for longer-term planning

Caution: In light of Bob's condition, they are tempted to step away from longer-term planning. He might say he doesn't have enough time for longer-term planning and put it on hold. Resist this temptation. Consider your legacy. Bob might just be thinking time is short. Bob might be right, but he might also be wrong.

If your finances have a long-term outlook and you live short, then it worked, although perhaps not in the way you wanted. On the other hand, if you have a short-term financial outlook and you live long, *ouch*. This does not work. Additionally, if you are married, your husband/wife and children cannot afford to have anything but a long-term plan.

Emergency cash *plus* known extras establish your short-term deposit requirements. Once you establish this amount, the rest needs to go into a long-term plan.

Additionally, if you are married, your husband/ wife and children cannot afford to have anything but a long-term plan.

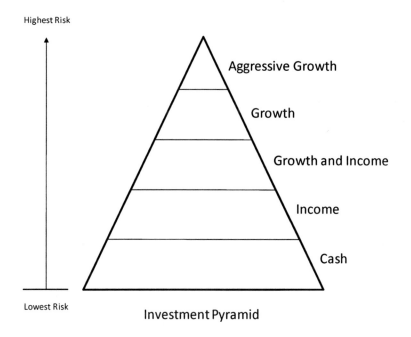

Investment Pyramid

Start at the bottom and work your way up.

Investment Pyramid
Here is the standard Investment Pyramid. The pyramid divides into five sections. Short term, low risk investments are at the bottom of the pyramid and aggressive, high risk investments are at the top.

Cash is king, but it doesn't multiply if not put to use. In the short run, cash is very comfortable. Let's say you have a $100 bill in your pocket. If the market crashes, no problem, you still have your money. The problem in the long run, you still have a $100 bill, and now it is worth less (because of inflation). You have been hurt by your $100 bill because cash doesn't grow.

Moving up the pyramid, you see the *Income* category where we find bonds, bond mutual funds, CDs, and other investments primarily focused on generating income. It might be very comfortable to put the majority of our assets here. However, bonds are not designed to grow. A $100,000 bond years later is still worth $100,000 at maturity (with potentially much less purchasing power because of inflation). Putting all assets here will trap your income and you will become one of our "seniors on a fixed income."

The *Growth and Income* risk category is a "sweet spot" in investing. In this category are utility and other companies historically paying strong dividends, while giving you some growth potential. Yes, the stock prices in this category will fluctuate, but the up and down ride is not as shocking and over time, has outpaced inflation.

The *Growth* risk category is next representing companies on the move. Many of these companies are still expanding and growing into different markets. Companies like Wal-Mart, Home Depot, and Coca-Cola are still growing and looking for additional growth opportunities. Many growth companies are now looking beyond U.S. borders to find international consumers. This category fluctuates more as the market moves. Highs will generally be higher than the Growth and Income category and lows will generally be lower. Also, risk increases in this category.

At the top of the pyramid we discover the *Aggressive Growth* risk category, where you have the most risk. Here we find smaller companies still trying to become big, also we find international companies trying to compete with the big guys. Some of these companies may become the next great performers continuing to grow for decades like Microsoft and some of them will become bankrupt. The market fluctuations in the Aggressive Growth category are strong. When the market favors this category and those taking the risk, the reward is very attractive. When the market is out of favor, the downside hurts. You will see 20, 30, even 40 percent up years, but you will also see 20, 30, even 40 percent down years! The market ride is dramatic in this category and like an extreme roller coaster, not for the faint at heart.

Be careful. The portfolio becomes stagnant and usually won't change until you fill out the questionnaire again.

Most risk questionnaires (like the one in Chapter 6) generate a model portfolio with a split in the risk between stocks and bonds. You answer the questionnaire and your advisor helps create your plan and invest your long-term strategy. Be careful. The portfolio becomes stagnant and usually won't change until you fill out the questionnaire again. Yes, you will have periodic reviews, and certainly, your advisor will frequently review your investments. In addition, your advisor will typically rebalance the portfolio if beyond the stated risk. Although rebalancing is generally good, it might not be comprehensive. The Wayshak Pyramid®, in direct contrast, is *dynamic* and compels the advisor and client to constantly monitor (which is a good thing) time tables for the various emergencies and known extras coming up.

Wayshak Pyramid®

In my practice, I have expanded the traditional investment pyramid into the Wayshak Pyramid® and has quickly became a foundation for my clients. I hope it becomes one for you. Let me build the Wayshak Pyramid® for you.

Take the traditional investment pyramid and tip it over ninety degrees to the right. Now, put a time line through the middle. With the pyramid pointing to the right, the same risk categories remain; they progress left to right. As you add the time line, start with zero years on the far left, the base of the pyramid, and at every two years, move from one risk category to the next. At two years, you leave the Cash category and enter Income.

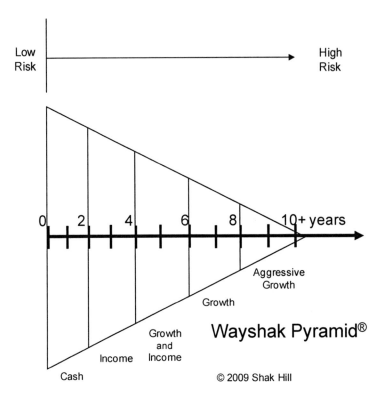

At four years, you enter Growth and Income. Six years starts Growth and eight years starts Aggressive Growth.

Let's walk through this illustration, starting at the left side of the pyramid.

If you need to spend money today, then you need to have the money in cash or near cash. Near cash is a money market/savings or checking type of account. If buying something today, you need to have money immediately available. Even if you plan to spend the money over the next two years, you still need to have it accessible. You do not have enough time to invest it (a major mistake many people make).

If you don't need to spend this money for two to four years, then you can generate a little more income from it. Generally, if you invest in a three-year CD, your money earns more interest than if you buy a six-month CD or just deposit your money in a money market account.

Note: As she did not have time for any other risk level, Ethel invested her cruise money in a CD. On one hand, keeping her money in the checking account would have been too conservative. On the other, moving her money into a mutual fund would have been too aggressive for the goal of this money.

Cut Time Line in Two Sections

In the following figure, you will see I have added a squiggly line cutting the time line in two sections.

> *The squiggly line is not straight because life constantly changes.*

The squiggly line is not straight because life constantly changes. On the left of the line are the Cash and Income risk categories. On the right, you find Growth and Income, Growth, and Aggressive Growth. The squiggly line divides the Wayshak Pyramid® in two sections around the four or so year mark.

As you begin to fund your plan, start at the left side and fill in your emergency cash and your known extras first. Once accomplished, you have now filled in the left half of the Wayshak Pyramid®, your *Short-Term Requirements*. You *must* have readily available money to cover emergencies, unexpected events, and normal life activities. You *must* allocate for known extras.

As you build your plan, fill in your short-term requirements first. This should allow you to sleep very well at night, knowing you have emergencies covered and known extras accounted for.

By design, I discuss these two questions with clients first: emergency cash and known extras. Once you know the answers, then fill in the cash needs and keep filling through the Income risk category as appropriate.

Only *after* you have filled in your short-term requirements do you have the opportunity to fill the right section of the pyramid for longer term

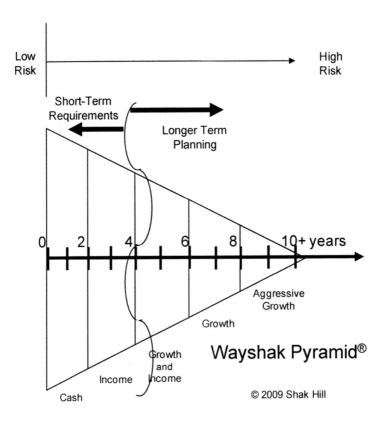

Only after *you have
filled in your short-term
requirements do you have
the opportunity to fill the
right section of the pyramid
for longer term planning.*

---

planning. You may not reach the Aggressive Growth category. Perhaps you will only get as far as Growth and Income. No problem. Nevertheless, most experts agree a balanced portfolio exposes some money to Growth. Now when you create your plan, you will feel more comfortable you have created it correctly.

Appropriate Risk for Time Available
Look at your goals and the corresponding "accomplish by" date. A man came to me a couple of years ago looking for my services and said he had two years before his retirement. Because he had inadequately invested over the years, he wanted to "go aggressive." He searched for the "hot stock" or the "get-rich-quick" strategy. As you can see in the Wayshak Pyramid® time line, since he only has two years before he needs to start using the money, he does not have the time available to take an aggressive growth level risk. I did not take him as a client because he wanted something I was not comfortable tying to provide.

This might be very true, but it doesn't mean they should pull out. It means they should hire someone to help them, even if just temporarily.

On the other hand, my clients Rachel and Andy came to me shortly after she was diagnosed with breast cancer. In discussing their financial plan, they said, "Don't worry about us, Shak, we're completely out of the stock market until this works itself out." They continued, "Things are

89

going to be too hectic around here for a while and we won't be able to properly manage this money." This might be very true, but it doesn't mean they should pull out. It means they should hire someone to help them, even if just temporarily.

Because neither one of them wanted to worry about the market *and* fight the cancer, they just sold out. I worry for them because in their late forties with their youngest son age ten, they do not have the luxury to sit it out until everything gets better. They have to take into account both their life plan and their legacy plan. Among their goals should be continuing to grow money for their son's college as well as retirement for at least one of them, if not both! When you study their Wayshak Pyramid®, you notice the family has many years to go before they need some of the money: eight more years until their son's college fund and fifteen to twenty years until retirement. Regardless of the diagnosis, they have a real need for continued retirement planning.

Note: Just because you have time, doesn't mean you must take the most risk. It merely means you have the ability to. For example, I have an eight-year-old daughter, Katherine, who has ten years before starting college. According to the Wayshak Pyramid®, I have the luxury to place money in Aggressive Growth, because that much time is available. This does not mean we *have* to or even if we *should* go aggressive, it just means we can, if we want. In contrast, when she only has five years to go, even if we *wanted* growth risk, the Wayshak Pyramid® would well advise us not to invest there, as we won't have the time, even if we have the desire.

Contrary to men, most women populate their investment pyramid correctly, from the bottom up.

Vast Middle

In the traditional investment pyramid, most men populate it from the top down. The Aggressive Growth category is the sexy one, where you buy and sell hot stocks. Here you take significant risk, which can lead to exciting cocktail party discussion on how much you made. When the market rewards aggressive risk, the stories about how much money is made begin to sound like that big fish that got away or the wonderful hole-in-one golf shot. Everybody loves the up market!

When the market punishes aggressive risk with a market downward turn, these same men grow frustrated. The conversation turns to women or anything but their losses. They end up selling everything, pulling their money out of the market, putting it in the bank and buying something else, perhaps real estate. They go from the top of the investment pyramid, jump over the vast middle and into the cash category. I start hearing, "I've lost money in the market, and I am never going to do that again."

Contrary to men, most women populate their investment pyramid correctly, from the bottom up. By populating from the bottom up, women fill in the cash category first with Emergency Cash. Unfortunately, they continue to focus on this category and keep filling. Like Rachel and Andy, they just keep buying CDs or end up overloading too much in savings, money markets, or checking accounts. Why do they do this? Because it's easy and comfortable. By not going much above the Cash or Income risk category, women often miss the vast middle as well.

With the traditional investment pyramid on its side and the time line superimposed, with most men, I have to pull them to the left, down their Wayshak Pyramid® so they don't take too much risk. Usually with women, I have to push them to the right to take more risk and grow their investment.

Look at this next figure. You now notice a new shaded area marking the "Vast Middle." The Vast Middle contains many steady, proven, long-term growth and income investments, often at reasonable prices. Investments in the Vast Middle held over time can generate capital appreciation and strong income. In addition, they tend to outpace inflation and preserve the investor's standard of living. As you create your plan, don't miss this Vast Middle of potentially excellent investments.

91

The Market and Medicine

I regard the market much like medicine: If you take your prescription correctly, two tablets twice daily, in a couple of weeks the medicine properly taken will cure your ailment. On the other hand, if you empty your bottle and consume all of the medicine at once, you will overdose and the same exact medicine misused will kill you. A similarity occurs in the stock market. If you treat the market correctly, your investments should outpace inflation and increase your standard of living over time. If you mistreat it and consume all of the risk at once, then the misused stock market will likely overdose and kill you.

When you treat the Wayshak Pyramid® as a planning solution, you will begin to create your long-term financial plan.

Add Back the Questionnaire

Once you have allocated for Emergency Cash and Known Extras, then you need to bring the results of your risk questionnaire to your Wayshak Pyramid®. Take only the investable amount, that portion for your long-term plan, and start filling out the pyramid. As your life changes and new expenses are identified, then immediately adjust your Wayshak Pyramid® accordingly. Congratulations, you have now created your dynamic investment plan. Work with your professional team to keep this current and connected to your needs and goals.

Here is the Wayshak Pyramid® with the Vast middle added.

If you treat the market correctly, your investments should outpace inflation and increase your standard of living over time. If you mistreat it and consume all of the risk at once, then the misused stock market will likely overdose and kill you.

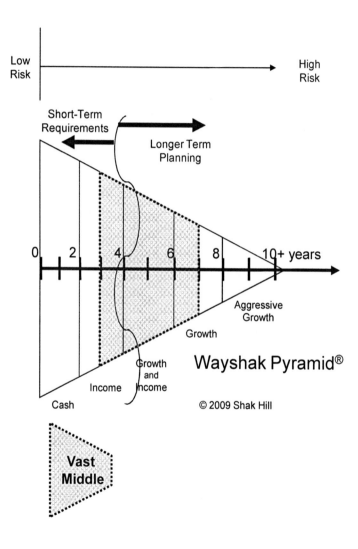

Note: The Wayshak Pyramid® allows all assets to be a part of one's portfolio, not just cash or securities. The Wayshak Pyramid® requires the client to place a real and objective risk tolerance on each and every asset owned. For example, a couple might own their own business and they are certainly very familiar with the business. However, they need to ask objectively, what is the true safety and security of the business? How easily could they sell it, or borrow against it for cash flow reasons if needed. How immune to business cycles of regular ups and downs is this business? They should consider all of these factors, and many more. After deciding, the owners need to place a risk objective to this asset. I dare say most, if not all, small businesses are Aggressive Growth risk. When you objectively establish the risk to your assets, then you need to populate the Wayshak Pyramid® in the appropriate risk category.

I have met with business owners in the past and they insist on taking diversified risk with their money, including the aggressive and growth level risk. Then we sit down and attach a risk value to the business (or the artwork, the stamp collection, jewelry, gold, real estate, and any other asset) and only after filling in the Wayshak Pyramid® with this in mind, we conclude which category needs to be funded and at what amount. If they score the business Aggressive Risk, then with cash assets, we invest around that business risk (as well as around the art, boat, plane, second home, stamps, etc). Once they score all the assets and position them in their proper risk level within the Wayshak Pyramid®, they can now invest the cash and investment portion of the portfolio. At this point, they will have invested all of the household assets in a proper manner reflecting the risk and time line they are willing to take.

> *Once they score all the assets and position them in their proper risk level within the Wayshak Pyramid®, they can now invest the cash and investment portion of the portfolio.*

Thoughts

Your financial plan needs to move forward. You have to plan for the long term even though it might not feel comfortable at the moment. To protect both your life and your legacy goals, you and your family have to plan for a longer time horizon than you may initially think.

Investors typically take either too much risk or not enough. Although the Aggressive Growth category is available to invest in, many investors shouldn't be investing at all in the Aggressive Growth category. You can (and should) take appropriate risk, based on time allowed.

Allocate for your short-term requirements first. Determine the amount of emergency cash you need to sleep well at night. Then establish your known extras from now through the next four years or so. Only after you have identified these amounts, then start filling in your longer-term plan.

You cannot create a long-term plan with only short-term investments. Short-term investments are just not designed to outpace inflation especially when you also consider the impact of taxes. Work with your professional team to create a well thought out, comprehensive financial plan: your plan for living and providing for your legacy.

You cannot create a long-term plan
with only short-term investments.

8

Important Insurance Review:
Connecting Past, Present and Future Needs

Financial planning encompasses much more than investments. Part of your planning right now requires a strong look at the insurance policies you have and to make certain you take advantage of their many programs. After getting a diagnosis, insurance options start to dry up, if not disappear entirely. However, you still may have some important options to consider. Many patients think after a diagnosis, why bother checking into insurance. In some regards, this may have merit, but in important ways, you cannot just ignore insurance coverage. Yes, because you have this diagnosis, you will not be able to pass a medical examination for many years (my wife Robin finally passed after eleven years!). Now is the time to check your existing policies for their benefits. You need to check on the *condition* of the policy and make sure it doesn't lapse without your knowledge. Read on and this subject will become clear.

> *Financial planning encompasses much more than investments.*

Note: A fine line exists when it comes to telling the truth and nothing but the truth. This line is delineated in the court of law, but is not as defined when it comes to business. No matter what, do not say anything incorrect or untruthful when discussing your situation. However, you do not have to *offer* information not asked.

Life Insurance

Do you know where your policies are? When was the last time you reviewed them? If you are like most people, you really never looked at them, even at time of purchase. They might be in your safety deposit box or they might be in some box in the attic. Take some time, search for your various insurance policies and review them. You may not have cared or even wanted to bother before, but life policies have many features you now need to be aware of. It may be well worth your time to have a meeting with the agent(s) who sold you the policy. Review if any changes are required or if any programs within the policy might now be to your advantage.

Applying For A New Life Insurance Policy

No hard and fast rules exist about when insurance carriers will cover a patient diagnosed with an end of life condition. Every situation differs, but if your premiums are high, you may wish to check into new coverage as soon as possible.

When you apply for a new policy, make sure you work with a qualified agent and ask for an "impaired risk" application. When you apply for life insurance, the insurance application always asks, "Have you ever been denied coverage?" You do not want a denial on your permanent insurance record. Remember, insurance applications are legal documents and you have to answer to the best of your ability and cannot be fraudulent. So how do you apply for coverage if you might be denied? Apply through the impaired risk program.

By doing so, you fill out all of the paperwork, but you will not *actually* apply for coverage. The insurance company will review the records and issue an opinion as to your eligibility for coverage. This opinion is not an acceptance or denial of coverage, but indicates a very strong guideline as to where they think your health rating is, based on your current medical condition, medicines you are on, on-going treatment, vital signs, height, weight and other factors.

By applying through the impaired risk program, if their opinion is not favorable, you will not have to report this as an official denial.

Jeff was a police officer and in top physical shape. Even with annual checkups, all looked normal with his health. It turns out that his stress level was off the charts and eventually he had a major heart attack. Through other events, Jeff ended up receiving a heart transplant. He now enjoys an otherwise healthy life and remains on daily medication to prevent rejection and infection of his new heart.

Wanting new insurance, Jeff applied with the impaired risk program and the insurance company has given unfavorable opinions a couple of times, still after year five from the transplant. Everybody's condition is different, so Jeff will apply again next year. He should not have to answer yes to having been denied.

If interested in applying, talk with your agent and start the process. There is no negative downside to it and you will learn from the insurance carrier how they view your situation.

Remember: Each insurance company has their own underwriters, those who approve or disapprove life applications. These underwriters base their determinations on studies and known medical conditions, like the universally accepted effects as a smoker on one's health. Although this can be the case, they each process other information differently. You may wish to apply to several carriers as one of them might cover you when others may have denied your application.

Term policies

When you buy a term policy, you essentially rent the coverage for a certain amount of time. Depending on the policy, most actually remain in force until age ninety or ninety-five. Even if you were forty when you bought a ten-year term, the policy probably continues much longer than you think.

The term policy works with the insurance company guaranteeing a level premium for a specified amount of time, for example ten or twenty years. Once the policy reaches the specified time, the guaranteed level premium expires and the new premium ratchets way up. If healthy, you would never pay this expanding premium and therefore let this policy lapse. You would just go out and purchase a new one for another term of ten or twenty years. However, now with the diagnosis, if your policy goes beyond the guaranteed level premium period, you will want to consider paying the new elevated amount. This will keep the policy in force throughout your life as opposed to just letting it lapse. In order to have all of the information to make an informed decision, contact the issuing company to get their schedule of premium increases, evaluate what your prognosis is and see what makes appropriate sense in your case.

The important lesson here is most term policies don't end after the level premiums end. Continuing a term policy with higher premiums might be an option in your situation.

If your term policy is scheduled to expire at some point in the future or if the premiums are going to ratchet way up, you may want to convert to a permanent policy.

Convertibility

If you have a term policy, you most likely have the ability to convert this policy to a permanent one. You normally can convert within the first ten years of issue without evidencing your medical condition. Give this some thought. Depending on your prognosis, you may have many years left to live. If your term policy is scheduled to expire at some point in the future or if the premiums are going to ratchet way up, you may want to convert to a permanent policy.

For example, let's say you bought a ten year term policy and in year eight, you receive your diagnosis. No one knows for sure the future, but if you have more than two years more to live, it may make great sense to convert the policy now, and keep the policy in force for the rest of your life. Without converting it, you might lose the coverage at year ten or be faced with expanding premiums.

Note: Some stronger policies have the ability to convert *and* have the waiver of premium (discussed below). This means you can convert to permanent status and when you meet the waiver conditions, the policy will make the premium payments. This can be a wonderful way to continue coverage.

Whole Life

Unlike term policies, whole life, or permanent policies have cash value and are designed to last your entire life. Term policies are designed to last only the period of the term, but the whole life policy will, like its name, last your whole life. In order to provide a lifetime of coverage, the policy builds up cash reserves to support the death benefit and this cash reserve eventually will pay dividends that can be used to offset the premium. The combination of a growing cash reserve and the increase in the subsequent dividends allow the permanent life policy to last your whole life.

Because of the increasing cash reserves, over time, the dividends paid may grow beyond the premium required, essentially allowing you to stop making payments and let the internal dividends cover the costs. In addition, the cash value is truly an asset to you that can be borrowed against, returned to you principle first and tax free (see your agent, financial planner or accountant for a greater explanation of this), or if you decide to surrender the policy, the cash value can be used any way you wish.

This illustration acts as the x-ray of the policy. Your agent will know instantly if the policy's health is in good shape or if broken.

Whole life policies offer some advantages that term policies don't. Two of them are listed below.

Automatic Purchase options

All of my children have whole life insurance I purchased when they were young. They have automatic purchase options allowing them to add coverage at certain ages without going through a medical review. At certain life events, like marriage, and at significant birth dates, they can automatically add to their coverage. Yes, they will have to increase their premium for the increased coverage, but if diagnosed, this increase in premium would be a small price to pay for the additional coverage. The ability to purchase this option is normally only available at issue. Look and see if you have this feature in any of your policies.

Waiver of premium
At issue, you may have bought the waiver of premium rider. If you purchased this waiver, under certain circumstances, such as illness, accident or disability, the policy will waive your need to pay future premium payments. This waiver continues until you no longer meet these provisions (because you became healthy, for example). If you have this rider, review the triggering conditions needed to activate the waiver.

Other Considerations

In Force Illustration
Most individuals really don't care about their insurance policy, and now diagnosed, I am sure there are many different activities you could be doing besides checking up on your policy. After all, you make your premium payments on time, what else is there? Plenty. The following discussion is vital and now with the diagnosis, becomes compelling. All permanent policies require the cash value to grow at a specific level in order for the policy to remain in force over your lifetime. We are not going into the detail here, but rest assured that it is the case. As potentially dull and boring as a discussion of life insurance may be, it just might be one of your most important activities to protect your family.

If you own a cash value policy, typically called "whole," "universal" or "variable," then you need to order an In Force Illustration. What is this? Glad you asked. Let me take this new concept and compare it with something you are familiar with. All of us can annually obtain a free credit report. We can also order a free report on the "health" of our policy. Ordering an In Force Illustration compares to a doctor ordering an x-ray of your policy.

For example, if you fall and land on your hand the wrong way, your doctor will order an x-ray to see what the condition of your arm is. Instantly he/she will know if you have a broken hand.

All policyholders will want to know if they have a broken policy. When asked, the insurance company must provide you with an In Force Illustration. This illustration acts as the x-ray of the policy. Your agent will know instantly if the policy's health is in good shape or if broken.

So how can a policy be broken? What might follow here could be a very technical discussion, which goes beyond the scope of this book. Without giving all of the technical reasons, the design and inner workings of all policies require the cash value be at a predicted and growing level throughout the life of the policy. If the cash value falls below where it should be, the policy will not last as long as you thought. Your agent or trained financial planner will be able to help you with this information.

> Let's say you purchased a variable policy and after making twenty years of premium payments added with the projected market growth, the cash inside the policy should climb to $200,000. Unfortunately, due to market conditions and poor investment performance, the actual cash value is $50,000. The level premiums you have been paying over the last twenty years are no longer enough to support your death benefit. If you do not have spectacular stock market performance ahead, the cash value will never catch up to where it should be. With internal expenses and mortality charges being increased annually inside the policy (because we are each year getting older), those charges will erode the cash value and potentially leave you with no cash at all. When this happens, your policy will lapse.

The In Force Illustration will show you and your agent if enough cash value remains in the policy and how long the insurance company predicts the policy to remain in force.

> *Silly example.* Wouldn't it be great if you had a car that automatically produced gasoline and you never had to pull into a gas station again? Imagine if that could happen. Down the road of life, the car keeps running and the gas tank never gets lower, in fact, almost magically, the gas tank level increases! Well, what would happen

to the life of the car if the component that automatically produced the gas quit making it? You would not know about it unless you had a tank meter (showing the "full/ empty" amount) *or* until your car completely ran out of gas and the engine stalled.

Think of the In Force Illustration as being a way to check the gas tank meter. You will want to know if the tank is at the predicted level, above it, or below.

Note: I have included in the Charts and Tables section an In Force Illustration sample letter you may wish to send to your insurance company. The report they send back will let you see the x-ray of your policy. You will know if the gas tank is full enough for the rest of life's journey or if the policy is broken and in jeopardy of running out of gas.

Work with your financial planner or your agent and have him/her order the In Force Illustrations on all of your cash value policies.

Add Money to Your Whole Life Policy

Strategy: The cash value inside your policy supports the death benefit. In strong policies the actual cash value inside will have outpaced the predicted cash level forcing the death benefit above the amount of coverage you originally purchased. The ability to have an increasing death benefit continues to be one of the fabulous advantages to cash value whole life policies. This death benefit increases *without* evidencing medical conditions. Therefore, you may be able to add money to your policy, boosting the cash value and in turn boosting your death benefit.

> *This death benefit increases* without *evidencing medical conditions.*

You are not be able to dump copious amounts of money to "go around" the normal increases in death benefit. If you do this, the insurance companies will recognize what is happening and will require a medical exam. To circumvent this, you can add incrementally during monthly payments, raising the benefit over time. The In Force Illustrations will provide you with the information needed to see if this strategy will work for you and your family.

Viatical Settlements

You can sell your life insurance policy to an investor who will pay you cash for it *now*. A viatical settlement represents a purely business transaction and a method to generate funds if you need them while alive.

Be cautious of the advisor who financially gains from this transaction. They may have a stake *to nudge you towards the settlement option.*

Caution: Financially, viatical settlements are never mathematically in your favor. If the settlement were in your favor, then the investor would be crazy to make such an out-of-favor investment. With this said, you may have important cash needs for you to consider a viatical settlement as this may be a last resort. Proceed with caution.

Here's how it works. Your policy will pay a known dollar amount at your death. For a discount of the death benefit, the investor will give you cash now and buy your policy from you. Viatical settlement decisions are complicated and are irrevocable. Proceed with caution and full understanding to see if this option has value to you. You would only generally consider this option if you were desperate for cash and this was one if not your last resorts.

Help: You can search the internet and find some helpful sites giving you information about these types of settlements. Be cautious of the advisor who financially gains from this transaction. They do have a *stake* to nudge you towards the settlement option.

Second Person Notified

Unfortunately, many policies lapse for lack of payment with the policy owner unaware of this action. Mature citizens have this happen far too often and safeguards are being put into place to prevent it, but it seems to still happen way too often. At some point in your life, you may forget to pay the premiums. The insurance company then tries to notify you. They send notices requesting payment and the consequences if they do not receive payment. However, suppose the policy owner is ill or in the hospital and fails to see the notices in a timely manner. If the owner does not make payments, the policy will default and be in jeopardy of lapsing. As a safeguard, I ask all policy owners to have a trusted adult added to the notification process.

With your diagnosis, you may want to add a second person to receive correspondence, statements and any important announcements from the insurance company. This way, if you become unable to respond or are just distracted from paying premiums, the second person will receive duplicate notices as well and be able to help avert a potentially disastrous cancellation of the insurance.

This way, if you become unable to respond or are just distracted from paying premiums, the second person will receive duplicate notices as well and be able to help avert a potentially disastrous cancellation of the insurance.

Understand Incidents of Ownership

Life insurance can be a wonderful financial planning tool. For premiums paid over time, your heirs will receive a lump sum at your death. This lump sum arrives *tax free*, which is the good news. The bad news: The IRS holds *your* estate accountable for the amount paid out, the face value of the policy. They do this when there is incidents of ownership.

In plain language, "incidents of ownership" means that you have material rights over the policy. For example, if you are the owner, or if you have the right to change the beneficiary, transfer ownership of the policy or use the policy for collateral, then you have an incident of ownership. You also have incidents of ownership if you have the right to surrender the policy and in many cases if you make the premium payments.

Why is understanding this important? Whenever someone dies, the IRS requires an individual's estate to be valued for estate tax purposes. If you have incidents of ownership on any life policy, then the IRS will add the policy's value back into your estate, even if the proceeds went to someone outside of your estate.

> You own half of your home, car and other joint property with your husband/wife. You are a partner in a business. You have a stock account, and you own a couple of life insurance policies, including the group policy at work. At death, the IRS requires all of these assets be valued together for purposes of establishing the net worth of the estate on the date of death value. The net worth includes the value of all life policies, *even if* the beneficiary of the policy lies outside of your estate, say your children, grandchildren, alma mater, or favorite charity.

Home	$375,000
Other Personal Property	$150,000
Business Interest	$1,500,000
Stock Account and IRA	$750,000
Cash and CDs	$250,000
Death Benefit of all Life Policies	$1,500,000
Total Estate	$4,525,000

Let's say your children are your beneficiaries. Your estate will be responsible for the appropriate estate tax and because you had incidence of ownership, the IRS will add back your life policies worth $1,500,000 to the estate for estate tax purposes, even though the proceeds went *outside* of your estate to your children. In all cases where the incidence of ownership applies, your estate becomes responsible for the estate tax even when your estate is not the beneficiary and did not receive the death benefit.

Get the Policy Out of Your Estate, if Possible

The inclusion of the insurance policy value can inflict a real liquidity problem to the estate. A $1.5 million death benefit could trigger nearly $700,000 due in estate taxes. If the $1.5 million did not go to the estate, (as in this example it went to the children) then the estate may not have the liquidity to cover the taxes. Your estate may have to aggressively sell other assets to generate the necessary cash to pay the taxes. When this happens, the estate may command less than fair market value as the IRS has a mandatory time table as to when the taxes are owed. Don't let this happen to your family. If you can, transfer the policy out of your control and into the control of another individual, like your husband or wife, or into a trust, like an Irrevocable Life Insurance Trust (ILIT).

By transferring the ownership out of your hands, the IRS will not be able to tax your estate for the death benefit value. However, precisely because of this strategy, the IRS does have the ability to look to the past for a period of time and bring back the value of the removed life insurance policies to the estate. The "look back" period is normally three years and increases to five when you move the policy to a trust.

Your estate may have to aggressively sell assets to generate the necessary cash to pay taxes.

What does this mean? If you sign over ownership of your policy to another person or a trust, you will have to outlive the "Look Back" period in order to escape the IRS's ability to tax your estate for this policy. If you pass away within this time, the IRS will pull the transfer back into the estate for estate tax purposes. Therefore, you have nothing to lose by starting the process.

Should you even bother with this technique with your current diagnosis? What if the prognosis is shorter than three years? Yes, you should bother. With improving treatments and medical advances, you may have more time than originally thought. Robin had six months to live seventeen years ago. One never knows, but I encourage you to plan anticipating living, not the other way around.

Caution: Because the IRS is potentially a big loser here, you need to properly follow many rules and laws. Your insurance professional or your financial planner can discuss in detail the "Transfer for Value" rules to make certain you don't trigger a current tax. Although tricky territory, the transfer can be accomplished correctly, but beware, there are many traps along the way.

> One never knows, but I encourage you to plan anticipating living, not the other way around.

Death Benefit Process

At an individual's death, the beneficiary should contact his/her financial planner to help with collecting the death proceeds. If you did not work with a planner, then contact the issuing company and find out what they require for death benefit claims. This process is fairly straightforward but each carrier will have slightly different requirements. Typically, they will need a certified copy of the death certificate, letter of instruction from the beneficiary and the policy (or lost policy statement, if you can't locate the original policy). You can help your family with some pre-planning in this regard by having all files and policies organized and accessible, and by preparing them for the transition so they will receive funds without delay.

Disability, Short and Long Term

You will want to review your disability policy and contact your agent or the issuing company to determine under what conditions the policy starts to pay. If your diagnosis prevents you from working, then you may be able to qualify for disability payments. If employed, contact your company's human resources team as well.

Long Term Care

Review your Long Term Care (LTC) policy to see under what conditions coverage begins and where are you required to receive treatment for the coverage to begin. In order for the policy to pay claims, some policies require you to be in a qualified care facility, while others allow you to be

108

in home receiving care. Some policies require an ambulance transport you first to the emergency room, then to the facility. Unfortunately, providers can deny claims if you drive your loved one to the emergency room. You will want to know what your policy allows and requires.

Generally, your policy will start paying claims when you can only do four of the six daily living functions. I will outline those here for your convenience.

Six Daily Functions
Without thinking about it, we all perform the six daily functions routinely and automatically. These are:

- Feeding – taking food from a plate and getting it into your mouth without help.

  Note: Someone else can prepare the food.

- Transferring – the ability to move in and out of bed or chair without assistance.

  Note: The use of a mechanical aide is acceptable.

- Continence – having complete control over urination and bowel movements.

- Bathing – the ability to bathe oneself or need help with only a single part of the body, such as the back or a disabled limb.

- Dressing – the ability to get clothes from the drawer and put them on, including fastening shirts, buttons and buckles.

  Note: Help is allowed with tying shoes.

- Toileting – going to the toilet and getting on and off the seat. Keeping genital areas clean without help.

Check with your agent to familiarize yourself with your particular provisions and to see if additional benefits are available.

Homeowners, Car and Other Insurances You Have

Review these policies and make sure your coverage is up to date for you and for the family. Verify the amount covered remains consistent with today's value of the item. If the home has appreciated (or depreciated), update appropriately. If the car collision insurance needs to go up, then raise it. Also, check with your mortgage company and see if they have mortgage life insurance, covering your mortgage if you die. You may not be able to qualify now, but there may be some nominal amount offered without you having to prove insurability.

Medical Insurance

Under no circumstances should you allow your health insurance to expire without consulting with an insurance specialist, attorney or financial advisor. Make sure you pay in full all premiums on time. With a diagnosis, you have little chance of qualifying for new medical coverage or it may become very expensive with many pre-existing considerations.

If you are under the company plan at work, ask your human resources office to give you the health care plan's summary plan description (SPD).

You may not be able to qualify now, but there may be some nominal amount offered without you having to prove insurability.

The SPD outlines the programs provided and how to file a claim.

You will also want to check the availability of open enrollment. There may be some employer benefits that now become more valuable to you than before. Check with your Human Resources professional to see if you are able to enroll and what programs you should apply for.

Changing Jobs

When diagnosed, what transpires if you or your spouse changes jobs? This is a great question and an important one. Under federal law, if you have continuous coverage from one health care provider, then the gaining company must cover you. However, the gaining company can rate your health based on your diagnosis, which will cause your premiums to be higher, and potentially much higher.

Additionally, most medical policies have a deducible and a co-payment until you hit an annual amount paid out for the year per patient and per family. Once you surpass this amount, then the co-payments end and the insurance company covers you at a higher payout level. If you change carriers, the new carrier will impose a new deductible with new annual limits. The new carrier will require you pay their new deductible. It is quite possible that you will have to pay out both deductibles and both annual limits if you change coverage mid-year. There may be little you can do about it, but by being aware, it won't catch you off guard.

One other consideration, you may find that the new coverage has a different network and the doctors that you are currently using may now be out-of-network.

Thoughts

As you check with different carriers and agents, look for provisions for disability, job loss, or other types of programs you might need. Outside of your home, your life insurance policy might be your largest single asset. Collectively, your benefits and other insurances have major advantages to you and your family. Don't leave any of your benefits untapped, unused, or worse, left to lapse. Don't forget to look at the Charts and Tables section to get a template for your life insurance review called In Force Illustration. A well-trained financial planner will be able to coordinate much of this work for.

9

Hidden Treasures:
Corporate, Fraternal, & Military Benefits

Many organizations have put together important programs for their members and employees. These programs exist for you and others when needed. Don't consider them a handout, but a hand up, for you and the family. You paid your dues and you have earned the right to tap into these benefits, especially in this time of need. Think of them as little treasures hidden away waiting for you. Go find yours.

> Through federal law, the ERISA Act of 1974 encourages and mandates certain benefit rules. Become comfortable with these mandates. Start with this web site from the Department of Labor: www.dol.gov/dol/topic/health-plans/erisa.htm.

There is a place for self reliance. When you work hard for something, you will enjoy and appreciate it more. In the process, you will become a better person for relying on yourself and learning the important lessons gained through hard work, getting knocked down with normal life events, and learning to pick yourself back up and press on.

However, this is not that time. This is not the time to be a hero. Ask for help.

For those of you working, schedule an appointment with your Human Resources (HR) professionals at work. Also, don't forget to check with your company's group health service provider. Your company probably uses a professional health agent who can act as an intermediary with the insurance carrier. These health service providers are experts in the field and can sometimes provide more detailed information than the HR team. Because the employer compensates health services providers, you will be able to use their services without expense to you..

If you have any concerns about how everything will play out at work, you may want to seek advice from a lawyer.

Note: Remember that HR is a representative of your employer. It is a good idea to have a clear sense of what treatments you may need to undergo and what kind of time off you may require before arranging a meeting. As with other situations, a prudent course of action is to relate information on a "need to know basis." If you have any concerns about how everything will play out at work, you may want to seek advice from a lawyer.

Corporate

When meeting with HR, find out what happens if your diagnosis prevents you from working. You may wish to ask the following questions:

> What happens if you become so ill you are unable to perform your employment tasks?

> Does this affect your company group life insurance?

> What about short term or long term care coverage? How about short or long term disability?

> If unable to continue working, what are the pros and cons of going on unemployment?

> What happens to medical coverage for your family?

Do you need to consider COBRA medical coverage? COBRA stands for Consolidated Omnibus Budget Reconciliation Act of 1985.

If eligible, is it better for you to retire?

When benefits are received are they taxable or tax free?

How much leave and sick time is available? Is it better to take the leave or sell it back if able?

Every work-related benefit package covers employees differently. A company could have several different programs depending on when you were hired. Are you "grandfathered" in? Pay attention if you had a break in service with the same company.

You will want to find the answers to the above questions so you don't leave any stone unturned and don't leave any benefit on the table.

Stock Options and Other Income Opportunities

Review the different stock options you have. Determine if you have Non-Qualified and/or Incentive Stock options. Depending on which one you have will dictate how they are taxed. Like anything else, the tax implication of stock options can be complicated. Below is one of the considerations you will need to make. There are others. Check with your accountant to determine the tax impact of any stock options.

One of the first things to do is to determine which ones are exercisable and see if any are "in the money." If so, consider exercising them now. The reason to do this now is because of taxes. Let me explain.

When you exercise stock options, the amount of the grant is taxable at your *personal* income tax bracket. This amount is added to your income and you will pay ordinary income taxes on this.

If you pass away holding stock options, your estate will exercise the favorable options, but the

You guessed it; the estate tax rate is more aggressive than the ordinary rates.

115

estate will pay the taxable amount at the *estate* tax rate. You guessed it; the estate tax rate is more aggressive than the ordinary rates. Said differently, the estate will go through the tax brackets faster than you would while alive.

Here I have included the current (as of 2009) IRC Table 1 for Married Filing Joint taxpayers as well as IRC Table 5 for Estates. These are the Federal IRS tables representing your federal income tax. Check with your state to see what their income tax tables look like. Be prepared to find similar results.

Note: In years to come, the tax tables are sure to change. Please use these tables as an illustration and contact an accountant for current and timely tax information.

TABLE 1 - Section 1(a). - Married Individuals Filing Joint Returns and Surviving Spouses[1]

If Taxable Income Is:	The Tax Is:
Not over $15,650	10% of the taxable income
Over $15,650 but not over $63,700	$1,565 plus 15% of the excess over $15,650
Over $63,700 but not over $128,500	$8,772.50 plus 25% of the excess over $63,700
Over $128,500 but not over $195,850	$24,972.50 plus 28% of the excess over $128,500
Over $195,850 but not over $349,700	$43,830.50 plus 33% of the excess over $195,850
Over $349,700	$94,601 plus 35% of the excess over $349,700

TABLE 5 - Section 1(e). – Estates and Trusts[1]

If Taxable Income Is:	The Tax Is:
Not over $2,150	15% of the taxable income
Over $2,150 but not over $5,000	$322.50 plus 25% of the excess over $2,150
Over $5,000 but not over $7,650	$1,035 plus 28% of the excess over $5,000
Over $7,650 but not over $10,450	$1,777 plus 33% of the excess over $7,650
Over $10,450	$2,701 plus 35% of the excess over $10,450

[1]www.irs.gov/pub/irs-drop/rp-06-53.pdf

Note: You may also need to consider the deferred compensation you have accumulated over the years or any other type of income you have not yet received. Under the tax code, the IRS never forgives taxable income. No income loopholes exist where one is able to shift income to another person. The IRS closed these types of loopholes years ago. Consult with your professional tax advisor to see if an advantage exists in you taking the income now or delaying it for your estate to take it.

By looking at the tables, you can easily see income has to eclipse $349,700 to reach the highest *personal* tax of 35%, but it only takes $10,450 to reach the highest *estate* tax of 35%. With only considering your tax situation, your financial condition improves if you exercise in the money options as soon as you can for taxable incomes below $349,700.

Important Consideration: When you withdraw money from retirement accounts, IRA, 401(k)s, and gains in annuities, the IRS never forgives the income tax due from these accounts (whether taken out by you or your beneficiary). A nice strategy due your consideration is that your beneficiary(s) has the ability to stretch your retirement and annuity accounts over their lifetime. The IRS still taxes the income, but the *delay* can be meaningful to your heir.

Life Insurance

Many corporations offer life insurance as an employee benefit. The amount of this insurance is commonly $50,000, as this level maximizes the amount an employer can write off on corporate taxes. Check what your maximum level is and verify you have it. For example, you may have a life insurance allowable amount up to three times your salary *without* having to prove your health status. If you are not capped out, when eligible, you will want to increase your coverage. Depending on your company's rules, you may have to wait for the open enrollment period. Either way, find out what is available to you.

> *For example, you may have a life insurance allowable amount up to three times your salary* without *having to prove your health status.*

> Pat wanted to save some money when he was first hired, so when he elected his life insurance, he took one times his salary as his company paid for this amount. Now diagnosed, he has the ability to increase his coverage up to his company's allowable three times his salary limit *without* having to go through a medical exam, even though he has to pay the premium difference.

Also when looking into your company life insurance, take the time to verify your beneficiary. Make sure you review in this book the discussion on beneficiaries when considering who the best beneficiary is for the goals you have. When you review page 66, you will see, for example, minor children are normally not good direct beneficiaries and many headaches can arise from this declaration. Additionally, avoid naming your estate as the beneficiary. If you do, then the death benefit will needlessly have to go through probate, and all of the associated fees, time delays, and court rulings.

Does your corporation have any consideration at your death? For example, the military provides some immediate cash assistance at death. Does your company have a similar policy?

Note: The reason you can get life insurance through work without going through the normal underwriting process is because you belong to a group of employees. Insurance companies will adjust everybody's premium in the group expecting some to be healthier than others. Don't feel like you are taking advantage of the insurance company or your employer by increasing your coverage. All associated members are entitled to the program. You would be wise to use it and your family will be better off because you did.

> *The healthy spouse needs to check with his/her HR department as well.*

Important: The healthy spouse needs to check with his/her HR department as well. Many corporate plans allow for the worker to cover the spouse up to some limited amount, *without* the spouse undergoing a medical evaluation. If you have not elected this option, do so immediately.

Short Term Disability

Most companies also offer short term disability insurance. Check with your HR team and find out at what point your eligibility kicks in. In other words, do you have to be out for a certain number of days (eight days is common), under care of a physician, in a medical facility, or can you be at home? Again, everybody's coverage is different. If chemotherapy causes you to become weak and unable to go to work, are you eligible?

> *Find out at what point your eligibility kicks in.*

> John is diagnosed with colon cancer and through some treatments and surgery, he missed work for six days. He called his manager and let him know although still in a great deal of pain, he would be back to work tomorrow. John's thinking was getting back to work would help get his mind off of the illness and get him back in the saddle.

119

Luckily, John's manager knew the company's short term disability policy kicked in after eights day of missed work due to illness. Because John was still under the care of a physician, his manager told him to stay home for two more days.

Since John has now been out of work for the waiting period of eight days, he does not have to meet this requirement again and would be covered by the company's policy if he misses work in the future.

You cannot be on full salary and collect disability. Most programs prohibit this, as you would then be "double dipping" with no incentive to get back to work. Coordinate with your HR team and the professional health agent who works with your company and determine if you go on disability:

How does going on disability affect your other coverage?

Does this affect your life insurance?

Does it influence your medical coverage?

If you retire, how is your short term disability affected?

Please make sure as you review your coverage, you cross check the impact on the other programs.

Thoughts

As you can see, the programs available from work will affect you in many ways. I strongly encourage you to trust, but verify everything you are told. Have the HR team back up in writing what they are telling you, so you and your family will have a reference point to work from. Be patient with your HR staff. Many of them are great when it comes to the daily functions of the HR position, but your situation may be new to them. Give them time to appropriately research your questions or concerns, but I would also give them a deadline that they agree to. With an agreed upon deadline, you will know your request is being researched in a timely manner.

Your insurance service provider may be a great resource to you. Ask the HR team who this individual is and contact him/her immediately.

Important: You can move the insurance you have from the company to you personally. You essentially go from a group policy to an individual one. You have a narrow timetable in which to exercise this move. Therefore, if you leave your job for whatever reason, you need to realize the clock is ticking to move important benefits. For example, group life insurance should be able to move without evidence of insurability within the portability period (around 30 days). You will not want to miss this opportunity. If you do, then you will have to re-apply and prove insurability, which you won't be able to with a diagnosis. Among others, check your HSA (Health Savings Account) to see if it is also portable.

For example, group life insurance should be able to move without evidence of insurability within the portability period (around 30 days).

Fraternal

Talk with the groups you belong to and see if they have programs you may be eligible for. Check with your church to see if something exist for members of the congregation; check with the Lions, Kiwanis, Rotary, Knights of Columbus, Veterans of Foreign Wars (VFW), American Legion, AARP, and so forth. There are many organizations that have programs you may be able to tap into. If nothing formal, certainly as a member of the group, you will have some contacts who can provide information and may even volunteer time to help you and your family.

You might want to consider joining some groups as well, even professional organizations. Sometimes new members become eligible for certain programs just for joining. Perhaps one of your local clubs might have the ability to tap into a group life insurance program. There may be a wait period of one year before insurance is available (to limit their exposure for those joining at contemplation of death). One never knows when the end will be, but if after the wait period, then your family will have additional resources it otherwise might not have had. Sometimes the positive mental attitude conveyed by organizations is also therapeutic and may help in your recovery.

> The Knights of Columbus organization is comprised of practicing Catholic men. Formed in part to offer insurance coverage for the bread winner to prevent family poverty, the Knights (as they are called) have grown into the largest Catholic fraternal organization in the world. As a benefit to all joining men, they have a no-medical, no-questions asked $5,000 policy. If diagnosed, you can still join the Knights and you will at least receive this coverage. (Programs change all the time so make sure you check before joining.)

Military

If you have served or are serving in any branch of the military, check with the military to verify your benefits. Even if no longer on active duty, there may be some programs available to help you and your family. Certainly if on active duty, in the Reserves or Guard, you have benefits available to you. Check with the Personnel Office to receive a complete briefing on those programs.

If you suspect your military time caused the diagnosis, like exposure to Agent Orange or other chemicals used during your active duty time, you may also be eligible for associated benefits.

Make sure to check with the Veteran's Administration as well. If you suspect your military time caused the diagnosis, like exposure to Agent Orange or other chemicals used during your active duty time, you may also be eligible for associated benefits. When you contact them, have your Report of Separation Form DD 214 available for their review.

If you are requesting a military burial or military honors of any kind, start requesting them as soon as you can. For example if you want a 21 gun salute, honor guard, a fly-over or other distinction, start coordinating now. For a burial in a national cemetery, work quickly. National cemetery requests are increasing and fewer and fewer opportunities remain. Better to request it and not need the honors, than the other way around.

Other

Look for any program you can find from any organization you belong to (or could belong to). Look at your alma mater, and professional associations. Even your credit card company might have some kind of program. Leave no stone unturned because, no matter how small, programs may be available for you and your family to take advantage of.

Thoughts

You do not want to miss opportunities available to you either through work, military, or organizations you belong to or could belong to. These programs are designed to be used. You are entitled. Take advantage of them for you and your family.

Note: Make sure you look in the Resources section at the end of this book for important contact information.

10

Creating Your
Professional "A" Team

There is a natural tendency to turn to friends and family members in times of stress, but the financial world continues to be too complicated to accept advice from people who are not experts, especially if you have a large sum of money.

In my practice, I have seen very well intentioned advice eventually cost the receiver unintended fees, angst and lost opportunity. With the diagnosis, your life may have just become more complicated and more uncertain. You can find great relief in hiring the right people to be on your team. If the estate is straightforward, you may only need an attorney and financial advisor. However, with a complicated estate, you may need to add a CPA and insurance professional as well as a trust officer and others. In any event, all professionals should be able to guide you through the process, making the complicated situation easier and helping you avoid costly common mistakes. Here are some considerations for you while creating your "A" team.

Looking for the Light

You and your husband/wife may never have used a professional in the past. Perhaps you filed your own taxes, did your own investments, and never thought much about hiring someone to help. Your diagnosis has just forced you on an unwelcomed path. Where the path takes you, no one really knows. How long the path will last is a mystery. Now is the time to consider seeking professional help.

Consider the following sobering thought:

> *A small mistake with a small amount of money results in a small penalty.*
>
> *The exact same small mistake with a large amount of money results in a large penalty.*

The court system doesn't care if an estate document is ninety percent correct. If ten percent wrong, the court can throw out the whole document! Unfortunately, the federal government lets us make financial mistakes. They also allow citizens *not* to take advantage of financial benefits available within current law. They do not give advice; they just collect taxes.

They also allow citizens not *to take advantage of financial benefits available within current law.*

Making Informed Decisions

You need to have a firm understanding of your current financial position. A Net Worth worksheet is included in the Tables and Charts section. Also included are an assets and liabilities worksheet and a cash flow analysis. Once you know your financial condition, you need to start assembling your professional team.

Here is a discussion in detail regarding the different advisors you will want on your team, what their qualifications should be, and how they will be able to help you, as well as some questions you will want to ask them.

Attorney

Most likely, after you receive your diagnosis, one of your first appointments will need to be with an estate planning attorney. Let's discuss the estate planning attorney's qualifications, role and compensation, as well as the basic question as to when you need one.

125

What Are Their Qualifications?

While an attorney must pass the bar to practice law, many states do not have strict requirements or formalized licensure for specialty fields like "estate planning" or "real estate" law. While many lawyers engage in ongoing continuing legal education, it is always a good idea to do some research or get a referral.

When you need professional services, look for professional accomplishments and ongoing expertise in that field. For example, if you were going to have a baby, you would look for a medical doctor who had specialized training and education in the area of obstetrics and gynecology. When looking for an attorney, confirm that the attorney has relevant experience, formal education and certification in that field.

Not all attorneys are educated alike. Look for a good educational background and experience in the field of estate planning. When it comes to large taxable estates, I encourage you to consider an attorney with an LL.M. (Master in Laws) degree in taxation. The LL.M. degree compares to an MBA in business and management disciplines. This degree should provide additional expertise with a taxable estate and knowledge helping the attorney identify potential taxation issues and prevent costly mistakes.

When it comes to large taxable estates, I encourage you to consider an attorney with an LL.M. (Master in Laws) degree in taxation.

An estate planning attorney should do at least fifty percent of his/her work in the estate planning field. For more complicated estates, seek an attorney who exclusively deals with estate planning. I personally would hesitate going to an attorney who can help me (a) sue my neighbor, (b) divorce my wife, (c) sell my home, and, oh by the way, (d) create my estate planning documents.

Although no hard-and-fast rule exists, it requires time and experience for an attorney to fully understand the ever-changing estate laws. The qualified attorney has to know what you, as the client, are really looking

126

to do. He/she should have the experience and ability to translate your wishes into a correctly executed document that others will honor and act upon after your death, in exact accord with your wishes. A skilled estate planning attorney will understand the law – that is a given – but will also know which questions to ask and pitfalls to avoid.

Just knowing the law isn't enough. There needs to be real world experience to ensure your plan works the way you want it to. Don't feel embarrassed to ask:

> How many documents per month is the attorney creating?
>
> How many years has the attorney been in this field? (not just how long has he/she been an attorney)
>
> In what other areas of law does the attorney practice?

After all, your legacy rests in part with the lawyer who creates documents within the confines of words on a piece of paper. You have a right to know the answers to these questions.

An established estate planning attorney may have been awarded a "board certified" distinction. An attorney can hold him/herself to be board certified in estate planning only after years of experience and demonstration of technical expertise in the field. The hiring of a board certified estate planning attorney becomes vital for more complicated estates and certainly doesn't hurt for any level of estate planning.

Note: Not all states have board certified designations.

The American College of Trust and Estate Counsel (ACTEC) is an outstanding source when researching the credentials of your attorney. ACTEC was created to allow estate planning professionals a venue for excellence in estate planning. According to their web site, www.actec.org, the purpose of the organization is,

"To maintain an association, international in scope, of lawyers skilled and experienced in the preparation of wills and trusts; estate planning; probate procedure and administration of trusts and estates of decedents, minors and incompetents; to improve and reform probate, trust and tax laws, procedures, and professional responsibility, to bring together qualified lawyers whose character and ability will contribute to the achievement of the purposes of the College."

Another area to investigate is your local estate planning council. I belong to the Northern Virginia Estate Planning Council and was a board member of the Brevard Estate Planning Council when I lived in Florida. These local councils have dedicated professionals who receive year-round education and professional guidance. Check to see if the attorney belongs to the local council.

Every state has a bar association, generally located in the capital city. Contact the bar association and ask for a directory of estate planning attorneys (attorneys who have self reported they practice in estate planning). This list proves to be a helpful start.

What is the Attorney's Role?

The attorney legally protects you and clearly expresses your wishes through documents, within the laws of the state where you live. Make sure you mention if you own property in other states. Your attorney may be licensed in other states or can provide you with a referral. The coordination of this effort will be important to you.

> *The attorney legally protects you and clearly expresses your wishes through documents, within the laws of the state where you live.*

Make sure the attorney translates all the legal jargon for you. The attorney may provide you with a cover page on your estate planning documents spelling out in plain English what the documents say. The legal terminology is important to pass statutory regulation, but you may want to give strong consideration to creating your own summary document, no more than a couple of pages, explaining in your own words what your decisions are and why you made them.

Do You Really Need an Attorney?

Because so much information exists on the Internet, you can find just about anything there, including estate planning forms. If not on the Internet, books galore are available for checkout at the library and are helpful in creating your own estate planning documents.

Proceed very cautiously if you embark on a do-it-yourself approach.

In the estate planning and probate process, a good attorney knows what to do, when to do it, and can do properly do it so much faster than you can. If the attorney makes a mistake, then he or she becomes professionally liable to fix it at no cost to you. If you make a mistake by doing it yourself, you may spend money many times over by having an attorney come behind you and clean it up.

Remember your legacy if you decide to create your own estate planning documents. With one thing invalid in your documents, the court could throw out the entire document.

Remember your legacy if you decide to create your own estate planning documents. With one thing invalid in your documents, the court could throw out the entire document. Your will might be invalidated for some innocuous reason like not being properly witnessed. If your will is thrown out, then your estate will be governed by your state's intestacy laws (this being one of the least desirable ways to transfer assets).

> I knew a smart man who had a PhD and was very computer savvy. He was a do-it-yourself kind of guy who didn't want to pay for legal help. He downloaded the estate

forms but never acted on them. He died suddenly of a heart attack. Nothing was signed. Nothing was executed within the law. The major complication was this was his second marriage. He had children from both marriages, and there was no direction about his estate. The legacy he left was not the one he had intended.

How Are Attorneys Paid?

Many attorneys charge a flat fee to create the documents you need. After the initial consultation (which is usually free), they should let you know what documents you need and what the fee will be. Some will charge by the hour, so make sure you get a strong estimate as to how many hours it will take.

In the selection process, be mindful of expenses but don't make your decision based solely on them. Your situation dictates the skill and knowledge you require and, consequently, the cost. If you get someone who specializes in estate planning, he or she will most likely spend less time having to learn what to do than someone else who will charge less per hour, yet take more hours.

Financial Advisor

In addition to hiring an attorney, the other professional you will want on your team is the financial advisor. Defining "financial advisor" is a little tricky so I need you to stay with me regarding the explanation.

With the mention of the word "teacher," what comes to mind? You might think about your favorite piano teacher, or, if like my daughter Katherine, she thinks of her favorite 2nd grade teacher. You may have even thought of your college days and your professor who help guide you, or for me, that obnoxious instructor pilot who liked to yell, yet saved my life more than once. Perhaps you substituted the word coach, mentor, professor, or educator. The word teacher can mean so many things to each of us.

To carry this further for just a second, how would you explain the qualifications of a teacher? I guess to teach piano, one would need to know the keys, but no controlling authority grants piano teaching licenses. How about for your coach, mentor, professor, instructor pilot and educator? There are myriads of expertise, personal touch, techniques, listening skills, motivation, certificates, academics and other traits that you might use when explaining to me the qualifications of a teacher.

Just like there are many types of teachers, there are many types of financial advisors. You may receive financial advice from an attorney, a Certified Public Accountant (CPA), insurance agent, banker, or trust officer. You can even get advice by purchasing a magazine or book and even through watching TV shows.

Perhaps this seemingly simple request just became very complicated without really thinking about it. The same complication is true with trying to define a financial advisor. (Just to make it fun, even a financial advisor is a teacher at important levels.)

Note: For our discussion here, I am generally going to speak about the generic "financial advisor" or "financial planner."

What are their qualifications?

You will be surprised to know *very few* formal qualifications are required in order to call oneself a financial advisor. The financial industry does not heavily regulate as to *what* makes someone a "financial advisor" or "financial planner."

As you know, doctors and lawyers have clearly defined requirements. Your state admits individuals to practice medicine and law. For the public school teacher, each state has teaching certificates and other requirements. Your state does not register financial advisors.

> *You will be surprised to know* very few *formal qualifications are required in order to call oneself a financial advisor.*

The authority for practicing in the financial arena comes from the Financial Industry Regulatory Authority (FINRA). FINRA clearly defines the requirements for the qualifying exams they administer. Even with this oversight, you still have to do your homework, as not all financial advisors are the same. They have a web site for your use, www.finra.org.

The threshold to entry for a lawyer and doctor are considerably high. The threshold for a financial planner is much lower. Yes, a financial advisor has to pass certain tests and maintain minimum continuing educational standards, but FINRA does not require any formal academic degree program. The financial advisor is not even required to have graduated from high school, let alone college. The similarity ends once you pass the necessary FINRA exam and become a "registered representative" to transact financial business. You have to research each financial advisor's education, background, experience, and other qualifications.

What is the Financial Advisor's Role?

In my opinion, when you look for help with finances, look for someone who takes a comprehensive approach to your financial situation.

When you hire your financial advisor, look at this person as your coach and quarterback. I often tell clients I am like a wedding planner. I don't bake the cake, but I figure out which one suits you best. I am also a little like your doctor. Your doctor doesn't make the penicillin, but knows when to give you a shot, where to give it to you and what to do with an allergic reaction. I don't make the investments, but after learning what your goals are, I figure out which one helps you potentially achieve it. If you have an allergic reaction and the investment doesn't work out, then we get a different one, always with your goals in mind.

The financial advisor's role is to work with your goals and dreams and help you select the solutions that will help you achieve them.

I don't make the investments, but after learning what your goals are, I figure out which one helps you potentially achieve it.

Do You Really Need a Financial Advisor?

Here's where we see the difference between advice and wisdom. Occasionally I get the question, "Why do people pay you for advice? I can get it by watching the TV or by calling into some talk show on the radio for free." My answer is always the same, *"Their* job is to sell commercials and advertising space. *My* job is to work directly with you and your financial goals. They don't know anything about you, your dreams, your passions or your fears."

In reality, everybody can give you advice: magazines, web sites, your next-door neighbor, and your son-in-law are all potential sources.

Webster's dictionary tells us *advice* means "recommendation regarding a decision or course of conduct" whereas *wisdom* means "knowledge, insight, [and] judgment."

Only when information is interpreted to your specific needs, coupled with formal education, excellence, and integrity, is wisdom *present.*

In the world today, information and opinions are everywhere making it very difficult to know if something applies to you or not. From twenty-four-hour news sources to "Your Money" segments on every news broadcast to CNBC displaying the time to the hundredths of a second, information and advice can be found everywhere you turn. Only when information is interpreted to your specific needs, coupled with formal education, excellence, and integrity, is *wisdom* present. Wisdom to support you, serve you, and make certain your plan accomplishes what *you* want to accomplish, not what *they* want to sell you.

Anyone can recommend, however dedicated professionals can give you knowledge, insight, and judgment. Some in the industry have passed a few tests and are more salesmen focused on their own revenue and others in the media are providing entertainment. You should have a consultant focused on investing as a means to meet your specific financial needs. When you hire a financial advisor, demand wisdom, not advice.

I heard a joke not too long ago bringing home the point.

> A granddaughter asked her grandmother, "How old are you?" The grandmother answered with a smile, "I don't give my age out and I am not going to start by telling you." Well, the granddaughter squared her shoulders, puffed out her chest a bit and said with a little pride, "Grandmother, I know how old you are. You see, I was just in your bedroom, and I noticed on your bureau you had your purse. Inside your purse I found your driver's license. Your license tells me a lot about you. It tells me the color of your hair, the color of your eyes, and your height. It even tells me how much you weigh. And, if I take your birthday and subtract it from today, well I know you're sixty-three years old."
>
> The grandmother answered, "Well, quite true."
>
> The granddaughter just shook her head side-to-side and said, "But Grandmother, I was so disappointed to learn you received an *F* in sex."

This joke becomes a great example of information with no wisdom. The difference is real and you deserve wisdom.

How Do Financial Advisors Provide Service?

As with anything, you have to pay for good service, and a financial advisor is no different. Different levels of service are available and normally, they fall into one of three service categories. The best way to illustrate the different service levels is for you to consider changing the oil in your car. Generally, you choose only one of three different ways to change the oil:

> 1. The cheapest way is to change the oil yourself. You have to know how to do all of the work, do it correctly and properly dispose of the oil.

2. You can go to a discount location and hope the attendant had proper training. You also have to hope he actually does what he says he is going to do and what you paid him to do.

3. You can go back to the dealership where you get an ASE certified mechanic and the backing of the dealership. If you have a service plan with them, they will call you to remind you to get the oil changed. They may even pick up your car and drop it back off.

Which one of these methods is going to give you the best service? Which one will be working with you about the overall performance of your vehicle? Which one cares most about your business? Which one knows your name?

I equate these three ways to change your oil to the service available from financial advisors.

1. You can do it yourself. Go online and make all of the decisions.

2. You can use a discount brokerage and they will help you get into the market. Most likely they will not be able to give you advice let alone wisdom about your situation. They will just direct you to their web site and the tools and calculators available there.

3. You can use a full-service financial advisor. This person knows you and your goals. In many cases, he/she will be able to give specific advice based on your unique needs. You will pay a fee or commission of some kind for the professional services you receive.

Which one of these professionals is going to give you the best service? Which one will be working with you about the overall performance of your financial plan? Which one has a personal stake in your success? Which one knows you by name?

How Do They Get Paid?

One of the most frequent complaints I hear from investors regarding my industry is, "My financial advisor never calls me unless he is trying to sell me something." This may be true, if your advisor is paid by the transaction. In the hiring process, you will want to know how the advisor is paid.

Generally, there are two ways financial advisors charge for their services.

1. The traditional way is through a transaction charge. This charge is assessed at the moment of every buy and sell of the different investments that you purchase.

2. The other option is through a fee for the level of service that you select. Generally a fee based financial advisor gets paid in one of three ways: hourly charge, plan charge, or fee-based charge.

- *Hourly charge*: Some financial advisors charge hourly. Be certain to know how much they charge per hour and approximately how many hours your plan and ongoing support should take. If the planner has strong industry experience, he or she should be able to give you an accurate estimate as to what the total expense should be. Make certain you understand this going in, and what the policy is if the estimated hours are exceeded. This financial advisor will typically provide a plan based on your existing assets, your goals, and your time horizon.

- *Plan charge:* Some financial advisors charge a flat fee for a plan. During the intake, the planner will get all of your personal data. Once he/she has this data, the planner will know your financial position. The more complicated your finances are, understandably, the higher the charge. When completed, the planner will walk you through the plan and recommendations.

Although you are free to go to others to implement the recommendations, sometimes this type of planner will welcome the opportunity to implement them through his/her services. The overall price of the plan may even be reduced if he/she implements some or the entire plan.

- *Fee-based*: Some financial advisors will offer the written plan as a courtesy with the expectation of implementing the entire plan when the process is completed. This planner charges a fee based on the amount of money invested and manages your accounts according to your plan. Under this pricing arrangement, expect ongoing communications and updates of the plan at no additional expense to you. You would continue to employ this planner as long as services rendered added value. Many clients like this approach because not only do they get a strong plan but they can implement it with the same person.

When you hire a financial advisor, find someone with strong credentials, experience, and a burning desire to help you accomplish your goals.

Professional Designations

What else can you look for?

Academic accomplishments

Undergraduate degree (Finance-related field preferred)

Graduate degree (Finance-related field preferred)

Professional designations within the industry

CERTIFIED FINANCIAL PLANNER™, CFP®

Chartered Life Underwriter, CLU®

Chartered Financial Consultant, ChFC®

Certified Public Accountant, CPA

Chartered Financial Analyst, CFA

The Chartered Institute of Management
Accountants, CIMA

Caution: There has been an enormous growth of "designations" in the industry. As anyone can create a designation, please be careful to research the particular designation you see. Many designations are out there, but only a few are well respected and represent industry excellence, which are listed above.

Note[1]: Some states are beginning to weigh in on the designations they allow professionals to use in their state. For example, Nebraska and Massachusetts have legislated certain designations may not be used in their state.

[1]www.registeredrep.com/mag/finance_achievement_bull_200708100523/

The industry has experienced an enormous growth in designations with more popping up. Here is a discussion on the most respected ones.

CERTIFIED FINANCIAL PLANNER™ (CFP®)[2]

Probably the best known and most recognizable designation in the financial planning arena is the CERTIFIED FINANCIAL PLANNER™ professional, the CFP®. The CFP designation was created in 1986 to set basic standards by what is now known as the Certified Financial Planner Board of Standards, Inc. (CFP Board). This Board oversees the CFP process which ensures educational standards, work experience, and ethical standards are met. The Board has disciplinary action available for professionals who no longer meet the standards, or by action, have no longer earned the ability to call themselves CFP professionals.

To earn the CFP designation, the candidate must pass comprehensive educational classes in:

- General Principles in Financial Planning
- Insurance Planning and Risk Management
- Employee Benefits Planning
- Estate Planning
- Investment Planning
- Income Tax
- Retirement Planning

Probably the best known and most recognizable designation in the financial planning arena is the CERTIFIED FINANCIAL PLANNER™ professional, the CFP®.

After completing these prerequisites, the candidate must pass a comprehensive two-day test covering these topics and applying them to several case studies. The pass rate on this test is 57 percent.[3] Additionally, the candidate must show evidence of hands-on work in the field for a period of three years.

In order to maintain certification as a CFP practitioner, the planner needs to accomplish continuing education, ethical training, and agree to abide by a professional code of ethics, pledging to conduct business with integrity, objectivity and in the best interest of the client. The web site is www.cfp.net.

[2]www.cfp.net
[3]www.cfp.net/media/survey.asp?id=9#link4

Chartered Life Underwriter (CLU®)[4]
The American College (www.theamericancollege.edu) confers this professional designation. The CLU has existed since 1927 helping families and businesses with extensive insurance planning. The CLU professional is highly educated through a rigorous program, has the required experience

in the field, and can provide a wide range of financial planning and insurance expertise. This professional has to meet continuing educational requirements as well as professional standards of conduct combined with ethical training.

[4]www.theamericancollege.edu

Chartered Financial Consultant (ChFC®)[5]

As the financial world became more complicated, the American College (www.theamericancollege.edu) created the ChFC in 1982 to further enhance the insurance professional. As important as the CLU is, the ChFC professional takes the next step by including financial planning, wealth creation and estate considerations. The ChFC has to meet strict continuing educational requirements as well as professional standards of conduct combined with ethical training.

[5]www.theamericancollege.edu

Certified Public Accountant

Candidates achieve the Certified Public Accountant (CPA) designation after passing the Uniform CPA Examination. This exam is given after evidence of an undergraduate degree in accounting or other related field. The exam is comprehensive and the pass rate is 31% of those who complete all three sections.[6] Continuing education is required as well as a pledge to conduct business ethically.

[6]Denise Flagg, dflagg@nasba.org, National Association of State Boards of Accountancy

Chartered Financial Analyst

The Chartered Financial Analyst (CFA) analyzes investment securities and overall portfolio construction. A CFA professional probes the detail of companies and works on creating investment portfolios. The CFA concentrates on individual companies and their products to the public. In order to achieve this designation, the candidate must pass three major exams as well as have three years of analytical experience. The pass rate for those taking the first test to those who successfully pass all three tests is 21 percent[7]. Additionally, continuing education is required as well as a pledge to conduct business ethically.

[7]www.cfainstitute.org/cfaprog/pdf/candidate_results.pdf

Here are other professionals you may meet.

Registered Representative

Most investors still work with the traditional registered representatives or stockbrokers. This professional generally works for a commission paid when they help you buy and sell an investment. Some stockbrokers are moving toward fee based financial planning, but many still operate on commission.

Bank Customer Service Representative

You will need to use the services of the local banker. When you walk into the branch, work with the customer service representative. All banks have them, but they are usually called something different depending on the bank. Some are Financial Specialists, Customer Service Representatives, Financial Service Representatives, or something similar. They are excellent sources to help you open the trust account, re-title accounts as needed, and conduct other traditional banking services.

Note: Many banks require their bankers to become licensed to sell investments to you. Although there is nothing wrong with this, if you have a financial advisor, make sure you coordinate with him/her before you buy an investment from the bank.

Trust Banker

Most, if not all banks, have trust departments. This fiduciary department manages money and provides other valuable personal services. If you name a bank as successor trustee, you will have a trust officer assigned to you. Trust departments offer a wide range of beneficial services.

Making Your Selection

Once you have decided upon your desired level of service and the expertise you demand, the time has arrived to interview and narrow down your selection. For each area of expertise you need, call at least two professionals and interview them. Ask the following questions:

- What is your education level?

- What are your professional designations?

- Who is your ideal client?

- Do you work with clients in our (my) situation?

- What are the total assets you have under management? What is the total number of clients you have? What is the largest amount you manage? What is the amount of assets you manage for your average client?

  Note: You don't want to be the highest account when he/she is learning from you. Additionally, you don't want to be the lowest, lost among higher level accounts.

- How do you get paid? (You know you will need to pay for services rendered, but you don't need to overpay for them.)

- How long has your longest client been with you?

- Who are your team members? Will I be dealing with you or with one of them?

  Note: Often someone is a "rainmaker" in an office, but once you are a client, you may get assigned to someone else. Nothing is necessarily wrong with this but you will want to know what to expect.

- Ask for references. When you get them, call them.

  Note: Consider working with someone who is younger than you. This person will most likely be able to support you for the rest of your life.

142

When you conducted the interview, did you feel comfortable? Did the explanations go over your head or were they at your level of understanding? No matter the credentials, the plaques on the wall, or the mahogany desk, make sure you felt comfortable with him/her. Chemistry has a lot to do with successful relationships.

Introduce Each Professional to the Others

Your financial plan needs to be coordinated. Now you have your team and need to make sure their individual efforts are collectively going to work as planned for you.

As you start hiring professionals to support you and your family, make sure they know about the rest of your team. Your lawyer, financial advisor, CPA, and insurance agent should be aware of the others. You may even feel comfortable having them coordinate with each other about your planning. In today's financial world, finances are more complicated than just one person or one discipline.

Your lawyer, financial advisor, CPA, and insurance agent should be aware of the others.

Joe and Diane always inform their attorney, Roger, on decisions I make with them. With issues I bring up, Joe and Diane confirm with Roger and the three of us send e-mails back and forth discussing their financial goals. We both know what the other is advising and how each piece fits with Joe and Diane's goals. What a great win-win-win for them.

Life Boat Drill

At one of my continuing education conferences, I heard part of our recommended planning process referred to as a life boat drill. What is this, you ask? Well, if you have ever been on a cruise ship, one of the very first things you do is a life boat drill in case of a disaster at sea. You have to put on one of those silly, bright orange life vests and then work your way on deck and stand under your assigned life boat. This serves several purposes.

One, it gets you to know you have an assigned boat. Two, to help you locate it. Three, you get to see how ridiculous all of your boat-mates look in their bright orange life vests.

Financially, have a life boat drill as well. With your team gathered together in one room, discover how each professional will support you and what each of them will do for you. If the time comes, who is going to contact family? Who is going to coordinate immediate care? How are the estate documents going to work? Who should the successor trustee and executor call first? Make sure you ask about all the other important issues unique to your personal situation.

This exercise is necessary, especially if you have a large estate!

Thoughts

Your professional team should be able to guide you and add wisdom to your plan, helping you achieve your goals and dreams. Make sure you hire the professional who fits with your personality and helps you understand the often tricky financial world. Do you need a professional team? I often save my clients more money than I could possibly bill them by not allowing them to make financial mistakes. Your team should do the same.

11

Explaining the Financial Planning Process

Your life has just become very complicated. As you enter into one of your life's most difficult periods, you will certainly have many struggles and challenges ahead. You might have friends, relatives and neighbors who will be happy to provide you with help, guidance, and opinions on many matters, even financial ones. While all will most likely be well intentioned, you may need to separate those opinions given out of knowledge and wisdom, from those that are not. You may face some very critical and time dependent decisions. I encourage you to review the planning process and see if a professional may help you in this stressful time.

How your assets transition will become one of the most lasting statements you make.

Many of these decisions will have far-reaching implications and will become the foundation of your legacy. How your assets transition will become one of the most lasting statements you make. After going through this book, you will be on the right path to achieving your desired legacy. If your legacy doesn't start for many years because you beat the diagnosis and the odds, then you will have your financial house in order for you to enjoy for those many years.

You need to develop your financial plan.

According to the Certified Financial Planning Board of Standards the financial planning process consists of the following six steps*:

1. Establishing and defining the client-planner relationship.
2. Gathering client data, including goals.
3. Analyzing and evaluating your financial status.
4. Developing and presenting financial planning recommendations and/or alternatives.
5. Implementing the financial planning recommendations.
6. Monitoring the financial planning recommendations.

* www.cfp.net/learn/knowledgebase.asp?id=2

Let's spend some time talking about each of these steps.

1. Establishing and defining the client-planner relationship.

When you hire and work with a professional, make sure he/she has a great fit with you and your family. This person should have advanced training and have established him/herself as being ready to handle your particular life circumstances. You may want an advisor who works with others in your situation, not learning as he/she goes. Financial planning can be complicated, so make sure you establish the expectation about the level of service and what you want from the relationship. Make certain you understand how the financial planner is paid and compensated for the advice and services provided. Establish the length of the relationship, perhaps a specific period of time or for the foreseeable future. Lastly, make sure you cover how decisions are made. Are they discretionary to the planner, or do you or your appointed representative want to be involved? There are no right answer here, you just want to know before you start the relationship.

2. Gathering client data, including goals.

Perhaps you have never been completely forthcoming with your finances before to any one individual: perhaps not even to your husband/wife. You need to lay everything out on the table. Don't hold anything back. Answer all the questions completely and thoroughly. Outline for your planner where and what all of your assets are, including all the hidden assets – like a Swiss bank account. Discuss your goals and what is most important to you. Don't simply say, "I want obscenely high profits with no risk." (Who doesn't?) Discuss your income requirements. Identify the assets earmarked to transition to the next generation. Mention gifting desires and legacy considerations. Discuss your goals, dreams and desires as to what you want your money to do for you, while alive and after your death. Your planner will also need to be aware of the legal documents you have.

Note: Most likely, your planner will not review these documents for legal considerations. Your lawyer does this. However, an experienced planner will be aware of these documents and should be able to identify if one is missing or needs updating.

3. Analyzing and evaluating your financial status.

The first step during the analyzing and evaluating phase of planning is to do an asset allocation to identify how all your pieces fit together (or don't fit). Your planner will collect the financial information from all your accounts and analyze them. The planner will group all of your accounts for this report. Your retirement accounts, brokerage holdings, CDs, money markets, checking, along with your husband's/wife's accounts will be combined into one report to see how they fit. From here, the planner will evaluate your assets and report the findings. This report will outline how much money you have in stocks vs. bonds, in international vs. domestic holdings, and much more.

In addition to all of your assets, your planner will look at all of your income along with your liabilities. The more thorough and complete you are, the better your plan will be. Once accomplished, you will have the information needed to move to the next financial planning step.

Remember: Be sure to include all of your handshake arrangements, money you owe, or money others owe you.

4. Developing and presenting financial planning recommendations and/or alternatives.

After evaluating your entire financial picture, your planner will be able to provide you with recommendations specifically tailored to your goals, dreams, and desires. Your planner will go over the steps needed to adjust your current asset allocation, if needed, and explain why this adjustment will help you obtain your goals. If you feel like there are misunderstandings or if there is a need for clarification, now is the time to mention them. Your planner will adjust the recommendations accordingly, so be certain you voice any concerns and make sure your planner is listening.

5. Implementing the financial planning recommendations.

To use the sports analogy again, the planner becomes your quarterback leading the team to move your "football" to your goal line.

Now is the time to implement those recommendations. As I mentioned before, your financial planner should act as your coach, coordinating the necessary solutions your plan dictates. Like a wedding planner, the financial planner does not do everything him/herself but taking into account your financial position, the planner should know which attorney, CPA or other professional to hire. He/She will work with your current professionals on your team, and if that slot is not filled, he/she will know of someone qualified to do the job. To use the sports analogy again, the planner becomes your quarterback leading the team to move your "football" to your goal line.

6. Monitoring the financial planning recommendations.

Now, you and your planner will monitor the progress. Together, you will review the process with periodic meetings and discuss the steps needed to adjust your plan. Again, as mentioned in the previous chapter, be aware of how you compensate your planner. There should be no surprises during this important process.

Thoughts

Review these steps with your financial advisor in great detail. If you do not have a written plan in place, you owe it to yourself and family to have one. The planner you hire needs to know everything about you. The information you provide may be more than you have told any one person in your entire life, maybe even more than your husband/wife. You need to do this planning step. Your legacy demands it.

Discuss important end of life issues and what your planner is specifically going to do to help you and your heirs. You may even consider bringing in the heirs to one of your meetings and start educating them on the inheritance. Again, you have the power to bring love and understanding to your legacy, or confusion and angst. Your financial advisor can help you facilitate this important meeting.

Now you're on your way, keep moving forward.

12

Money Saving Strategies

Let's talk about some strategies and ideas other families in this situation have used. Please choose the ones that make sense for you. Not all of them will, but you may find a golden nugget within some of them.

Gather, Don't Scatter

Over the years investors have been convinced that proper investing meant taking their money and spreading it out amongst several investment professionals. Over time, many investors accumulate, on average, four advisors and several accounts. From his 401(k), Roth IRA, Traditional IRA, brokerage and mutual fund accounts, to her 401(k), Traditional IRA, trust and saving accounts, a family can accumulate several accounts with several financial institutions.

This scattering of assets leads to a false sense of "diversification" by "not putting all of your eggs in one basket." Trouble is this strategy has really hurt most investors.

Three Avoidable Pitfalls

Many investors have unknowingly scattered their assets, resulting no one person managing or fully understanding their entire situation, goals or dreams. Without comprehensive planning, there actually is no real plan at all.

Without comprehensive planning, there actually is no real plan at all.

1. Improper Asset Allocation

Most clients come to me with their assets dispersed with several advisors and several financial firms. No single advisor knows what the other is doing and the portfolio is not coordinated. One advisor in firm A might be selling the very asset that an advisor in firm

B is buying. Unless there is one coach reviewing the entire asset allocation, then your money is not coordinated.

Your asset allocation should always reflect your current position in life, your current goals, future, feelings and family characteristics. When your hard earned money is scattered to other advisors and institutions, only you are left to properly manage your portfolio. Many are not trained to do this correctly and consistently and their overall plan suffers.

2. Improper Correlation Within Investments, Managers and Funds

Without it saying, each investment needs to be excellent on its own. The investment, manager or fund needs to have a strong track record (I like a ten-year record). You might be very able to select quality investments. Where the breakdown occurs is knowing how these investments interrelate. This is nearly impossible to track when one advisor is doing one thing, and a different advisor is doing just the opposite.

Let's think about a recipe analogy. You might have the best ingredients to make your favorite dish. You might even have quality chefs at your beck and call ready to make this dish for you. If you put all of these chefs in the same kitchen but don't let them know what the other is doing, a culinary disaster awaits. You can see that the likelihood of your dish coming out correctly is very low, no matter how good the ingredients were. Same is true with your investment portfolio.

3. Improper Monitoring of the Consolidated Portfolio

You know that life is not static. Your life is constantly changing. Whether it is your job, children, the economy, world events, new laws, unplanned expenses (and the list goes on and on), your world is constantly moving. Your entire portfolio needs to be dynamic as well. When market forces move, the properly managed portfolio needs to move with it. I am not talking about day-trading, but rebalancing when and where appropriate. Additionally, your goals, future, feelings and family characteristics are changing as well. Every day is either a day closer to retirement, or another day within it.

Having your assets scattered makes it nearly impossible to properly monitor your portfolio based on your changing life. With the technology and tools available, along with the new "open architecture" available at full service financial institutions, you are better off hiring one advisor to help you monitor your portfolio. This trusted advisor will coordinate all of your "eggs" and not put them in the same "basket." He/she can manage your diversified portfolio to meet your goals, future, feelings and family characteristics and make sure that your entire portfolio works in unison to make your dreams come true.

Note: In the past, many firms were limited to the solutions they could individually bring to the client. Many had their own proprietary funds or investments, which may or may not have been in your best interest. Today, full service firms have an "open architecture" and are able to go out into the market place and bring any solution to you that is appropriate. For your strong consideration, only hire an advisor who can go anywhere in the marketplace *without* limitation!

Gifting

One strategy often missed uses gifting techniques to lower the value of the estate. In the year 2009 and beyond, each person can gift $13,000* annually to any individual without triggering gift tax issues. I have six children so, in any calendar year, I can gift $78,000 out of my estate and my wife can gift her own $78,000. When we have grandchildren, my wife and I could gift to them as well. If you need to lower your taxable estate, gifting now can be very helpful.

* www.irs.gov/businesses/small/article/0,,id=164878,00.html

More gifting strategies are available by taking advantage of Section 529 College Savings plans. You can contribute to anyone who has a valid social security number! Federal law allows individuals to combine five years of gifts into a single contribution into any 529 plan. What does this mean to compress five years worth of gifting into one year? Simply, the donor can gift $65,000 ($13,000 x 5 years) *per individual* into his/her 529 plan. Not all 529 plans are the same, so you will want to be careful of the one you choose as well as the risk and expenses associated with them.

Note: After the fifth year, you can again gift five more years!

Note: Although you can gift to anyone, if you want to keep your gift in the family, the original beneficiary of the 529 needs to be a family member. This plan can be for you, your wife/husband, children, brothers, sisters, nieces, nephews, and still more.

Caution: You can't do both of the above mentioned gifting strategies. You cannot gift $13,000 outright to one person and gift all five years into the same person's 529. For example, if earlier in the year you gifted $13,000 and now wanted to gift into a 529 College plan, then your contribution can only represent four years, not five.

> As part of a normal gift, Grandpa Fred annually gifts to his only grandson, Fred the third (they call him Trey). To help maximize the gift, he gives at the beginning of the year. In the summer, Trey's parents created a 529 college savings plan. Grandpa Fred wants to give the maximum possible into this account. Because he has already given $13,000, he has used this year's gift to Trey. He can only compress four years of gifting for a total of $52,000 (4 years times $13,000).

Note: Either Trey (if age of majority) or the custodian of the original gift made earlier in the year can move that money into the 529, but not Grandpa Fred.

Opportunity: What if your grandchildren have graduated college? You can still open a 529 plan for them. Fund the plan to the max. When they have children, your great-grandchildren, your grandchildren can then designate those funds to their children. You can, in essence, create an education legacy from you to your heirs for generations to come!

Gift Tax Exclusion
If you have a large estate, consider giving away your applicable exclusion amount now while alive instead of waiting for your death. If you don't need the money, gifting these assets away now will also gift away any future gain or interest these might create or grow to. If you keep them, then they will cause an even larger estate in turn creating an even larger

estate tax. As a side bonus (which might have more meaning to you), those receiving the gift will now have it while you can see the enjoyment it brings and will start teaching responsibility and management while you can still help.

Gifting to Minors

Guardianship or custodial accounts have some advantages, but you may wish to avoid them as the asset becomes theirs at legal age, usually at eighteen years old. I don't know about you, but if I had had money at eighteen, it would have burnt a large hole in my pocket!

Consider using Internal Revenue Code (IRC) Section 2503(c) Trust For Minors*

Whenever you give a gift, the IRS requires the receiver have a "present interest" in the gift and the ability to use it without restriction. If you "get rid" of the money, the receiver has to "get" the money. Well, what if the receiver is a minor and you don't want him/her to get the money right away? An exception in the code allows gifts to be made to minor children now by putting it in a specific trust, without them having *current* access to the money. What's more, the code considers this a completed gift for the giver.

> *An exception in the code allows gifts to be made to minor children now by putting it in a specific trust, without them having* current *access to the money.*

The exception discussed here is *IRC Section 2503(c) Trust for Minors*. You can give money away now to minor children and through this trust, restrict their immediate access.

Three conditions have to be present for this type of trust to be valid. Let's briefly go over them but for more detail and to see if this works for your particular situation, please see a qualified attorney or accountant for guidance.

1. The named Trustee must have the discretion to pay expenses benefitting the child before age twenty-one.

Under normal conditions, eligible expenses would be for their health, education, maintenance, and support.

2. At age twenty-one, the child must have the ability to withdraw *all* of the money from the trust.

3. In the event the child dies before reaching the age of twenty-one, the assets must transition to his/her estate or be subject to the general power of appointment in his/her will.

*www.taxalmanac.org/index.php/Internal_Revenue_Code:Sec._2503._Taxable_gifts

If the trust remains in force beyond age twenty-one, the flow of assets rests on your imagination and requirements.

Remember: When gifting, you have important details to consider. Because of your diagnosis, do not delay starting the process as the federal government has built in time checks (like the three year look back) to potentially prevent your gift from escaping your estate – and the potential estate tax.

Still More Gifting Considerations

In addition to the 529 contribution or the normal $13,000 yearly gift, you can also gift for medical and educational expenses. You must make payments to the institution directly and not to the beneficiary.

Medical

You can make all payments for medical coverage, including health insurance premiums, but you have to pay them directly to the hospital, doctor's office, or insurance company.

Educational

Your educational gift is limited to tuition only. Room and board, books, and other fees do not qualify for this unlimited exclusion.

Example: You can give the annual $13,000 as normal or give $65,000 into a 529 plan *and* pay for all medical expenses including health insurance premiums, the cost of the cast, surgical procedure, medicine, etc, *and* you can cover the tuition costs, all for the same beneficiary. This can add up to be a substantial and meaningful gift as well as an estate reduction opportunity.

Warning: The tax laws may substantially change at any time. Make sure after any such legislation, you check with your planner to see if the new laws change your gifting strategy.

Appreciated Assets

To Non-Profit Groups

You can gift appreciated assets to non-profit groups like your favorite charity and church. For example, let's say you bought stock in a company years ago and its value has grown substantially. Consider gifting the stock certificate or shares to your charity and let them sell it from their account. This way, you get to write off 100% of the value as a gift for tax purposes and they receive 100% of the funds. Alternately, if you sold the stock, you would have to pay the applicable capital gains tax and be out the amount of the tax. When you gift to a non-profit group (like a charity, school or church), you give the appreciated asset directly to them. When the charity sells the appreciated stock, they pay no tax and both you and the charity bypass paying the capital gains tax.

To Individuals

This tax advantage does *not* work when gifting to individuals. If planning to transfer specific assets to your heirs, do not bestow it upon them while alive. If you do so, even one day before your death, they will not only receive the value of the gift, but they also receive your *original* cost basis. The cost basis is the amount you originally paid for the item. If/when your heirs sell, they will be liable for capital gains from your originally purchased price.

If you add them on as joint owner, for example on your home, brokerage account or CD, then you have *effectively* gifted to them. They now receive your original cost basis. This approach could be a costly mistake.

> George's wife Ellen died of liver cancer. At age 82, he recognizes he is slowing down. He is thankful for his good life and that his three children have all turned out well.
>
> Over the years, the estate has grown to just under $2.5 million.
>
> He has sold his home and lives in a nice assisted living facility.
>
> The brokerage account has always been "buy and hold," so many of the assets within have been there for several years and have sizable capital gains. George wants to place his three children on the account so they can help him as he ages. He also wants this account to transfer to them without going through probate.
>
> By adding the children on the account, he accomplishes the desire to bypass probate. However, he has essentially gifted the account value to them and the associated cost basis.
>
> At George's death, when the assets are sold, the children will report the original cost basis, triggering a very unnecessary capital gain tax!

Solution: Instead, considering taxes, George would be better off placing the children as POD (payable on death) on the title and creating a Power of Attorney if he needed one or all of them to help him while alive.

Business Strategies

Create or Update Your Buy-Sell Agreements

The buy-sell agreement identifies how you want any business interests you own to transition and creates the conditions by which your surviving business partner(s) will buy your interest at some established amount. This agreement has the ability to prohibit ownership of your business stock by relatives, employees, or outsiders, who are either inactive or incapable of running the business. By creating your agreement, you ensure management remains in what you believe to be the most capable hands once you no longer control the company.

> *Because you sign the agreement beforehand, your heirs sell your interest in the property at a pre-determined fair market value.*

Because you sign the agreement beforehand, your heirs sell your interest in the property at a pre-determined fair market value. You must have a business valuation completed *now* to determine and protect the fair market value.

Note: Have a fair market determination accomplished annually. Do an intermediate one when a significant discovery or event changes the value of the company, either up or down.

Have your business property appraised as soon as possible by a certified business valuation expert. This appraisal will aid in updating the appropriate agreements important to you while alive and the estate after your passing. You will want to look to a CPA who has the Certified Valuation Analyst (CVA) or the Accredited Valuation Analyst (AVA) designation because they are specifically trained in valuing businesses. You can learn more about this qualification at the National Association of Certified Valuation Analysts web site, www.nacva.com.

Consider Selling if a Sole Proprietor

In any individually owned business, you *are* the business. You have the expertise and the relationships. The clients know and trust you. Without you, the business quickly loses value as clients move to other providers.

You may want to sell or merge with a respected colleague in the industry. This merger allows coverage of the business as you go through treatments and provides a continuation plan for your clients. Merging or even selling might not have been in your strategic plan, but now is the time to reconsider.

It may be better to sell while you are alive. Experts in the field say the value of a sole proprietors company decreases about five percent a day when the sole proprietor dies.

Dilemma: If you sell while alive, you become responsible for any applicable taxes. If you die, your heirs receive a step up in cost basis, effectively eliminating the capital gains tax. You will want to weigh selling now at potentially top dollar and triggering a current capital gain tax, or having your estate sell with a step-up in cost basis but at a potentially devalued amount.

Some Tax Considerations

Note: Tax issues can be complicated. I am not a tax professional so be sure to consult with your tax professional when using tax strategies.

Allowable Deductions
Tax laws allow the estate to pay for certain final expenses from the estate account without subjecting these expenses to estate taxes. If you pay these expenses out of the estate, they essentially reduce the size of the estate and the taxes owed. Here are some of the important allowable deductions:

Funerals
Burial costs, such as expenditures for a tombstone, monument, or mausoleum
Cost for the burial plot
Cost for future care of a grave site
Other related costs

159

The estate administration
Executor's commission
Attorney fees
Accounting fees
Appraisal fees
Court costs
Other related costs

Debts
Unpaid mortgages
Other debt on property included in the gross estate

Paying the Estate Tax

For tax purposes, the total value of the gross estate is determined as the value of all assets on the date of death. The personal representative can select the alternate valuation date, which is six months after the date of death, if this date becomes more advantageous for the estate. Whichever date is elected, the entire estate is valued on that date. As expected, the IRS does not let us pick one asset to be valued at date of death and a different one to be valued six months later.

Why consider this? With recent large swings in the stock and housing markets, there have been major movements in these valuations. If a stock portfolio was worth $1,000,000 in the summer of 2008, six months later, it might have been worth $600,000. This decrease would have a major impact on the valuation of the final estate and subsequently the amount of estate taxes due.

You will want to review the entire estate picture when you consider which date is beneficial. Consult with your CPA or financial planner as to the best one for you.

Note: The estate tax under normal circumstances is due nine months after the date of death. You may have heard of "fire sales," when an estate tax is due but not enough is liquid money to cover the liability. In this case, the executor/rix has to sell assets in a hurry to raise the cash to pay the tax man.

Consider your Estate Liquidity

If you own a closely held business or other significant illiquid asset, your estate may not have sufficient cash to pay all the estate's obligations, including estate taxes, following death. Perhaps the principal portion of the estate may be the business itself. Without sufficient liquidity, circumstances may force the estate to sell a portion of the business to raise enough cash to satisfy these obligations. To help with this, the IRS provides a special tax law and the ability to create an installment payment plan.

IRC Section 303

A special tax law provision exists allowing for the redemption of closely held stock for the purposes of paying:

     1) federal and state death taxes
     2) funeral expenses, and
     3) estate administration expenses

If the conditions are met, the sale of these shares will be treated as capital gain, currently with a maximum rate of 15%, instead of being treated as a dividend, which is taxed as ordinary income and at a much higher rate. What's even better, as the IRS treats the stock as a capital asset, the stock will receive a step-up in cost basis as of the date of death. The taxable capital gain rests between the gain (or loss) from the date of death and the date sold. This can be a wonderful advantage.

Installment Payment of Estate Tax

If the closely held property is greater than 35% of the value of the entire estate, look into this provision. Your heirs will be able to delay the tax for five years, then pay the tax over the next ten years in installments. If you qualify, the installment program prevents a potential fire sale while keeping the business within the family.

Other Strategies and Considerations

Some of this information will be a refresher of earlier discussions, but it is included here as another reminder. You have many things you will want to accomplish, but don't overlook some of the oft forgotten ones.

Have Some Liquidity

Even with all the estate planning and important estate techniques, you may want to have a simple joint checking account with your husband/wife, or if single, with one of your children. Don't have too much in this account, but by having the account in the first place, your estate will have instant liquidity to pay for immediate bills and expenses without causing discomfort because the money was tied up in a trust or otherwise inaccessible for a time.

Safe Deposit Access

Someone else should have access to your safety deposit box. If no one else has access, the bank will seal the box and the contents become inaccessible until a court order allows it to be opened. If the key cannot be located, then the bank will need to drill the box creating additional and unneeded expenses to your estate. To that end, make sure the key is easily located.

Important papers

Make certain you account for all of your important papers and their location. You may simply wish to write down their location on a plain piece of paper readily accessible or you can use the refrigerator idea discussed earlier.

Hold Onto Low Cost Basis Assets

At death, the cost basis resets to the date of death value. If you have low cost basis property, then you may wish to hold onto these assets. Gift or sell the higher basis items first as they will have the least tax consequence.

Make Angels

When my wife, Robin, was going through her treatments, she didn't want to ask for help. She didn't want to be the one waited on, as she had always been the one doing the waiting. When we were in the military, she was always the first with the welcome package to newly arriving neighbors. Robin loves to cook so when there was a birth or an illness, she was there with a full meal for the affected family. Not wanting someone to dote over her, she was in a difficult position when she was the one with the illness. Being in need was uncomfortable for her.

I believe the homeless, sick, and the hungry give us all the opportunity to become like angels. Robin recognized that and as someone who was sick, she had the power to *create* angels. If she said, "No" to others wanting to help, then she essentially prevented them from fulfilling *their* ability to care for the sick. When she welcomed the comfort, or she said "yes" to a meal, then she allowed the giver to become her angel.

You may wish to accept your role as an angel maker and allow your family, friends, coworkers, church parishioners, and anyone else willing to help you become like angels. Accept the food. Accept the lawn being cut, the car being washed, and the house being vacuumed.

As someone being on both sides as the giver and the receiver, I prefer being the giver. When Robin was sick, her role changed from being a giver to being a receiver.

Your role has changed as well. You have an opportunity to give angels-in-waiting a chance to get their wings. Become a receiver and help make angels in the process!

Parting Thoughts

Life's challenges face all of us and part of those challenges includes our death.

You must take action on your plan and recognize there might be precious little time to work with. Simply going through the motions won't be helpful and not taking advantage of the time left, nor the important tax laws, would be unfortunate to you and your legacy.

Do you have any financial concerns? What are you going to do about them *right now*?

If she said, "No" to others wanting to help, then she essentially prevented them from fulfilling their ability to care for the sick. When she welcomed the comfort, when she said "yes" to a meal, then she allowed the giver to become her angel.

163

Charts and Tables

Net Worth Statement

Name _____

Date _____

Assets		**Amount in Dollars**
Cash - checking accounts	$	_____
Cash - savings accounts	$	_____
Certificates of deposit	$	_____
Securities - stocks / bonds / mutual funds	$	_____
Notes & contracts receivable	$	_____
Life insurance (cash surrender value)	$	_____
Personal property (autos, jewelry, etc.)	$	_____
Retirement funds (eg. IRAs, 401k)	$	_____
Real estate (market value)	$	_____
Other assets (specify)	$	_____
Other assets (specify)	$	_____
Total Assets	$	_____

Liabilities		**Amount in Dollars**
Current debt (credit cards, accounts)	$	_____
Notes payable (describe)	$	_____
Taxes payable	$	_____
Real estate mortgages (describe)	$	_____
Other liabilities (specify)	$	_____
Other liabilities (specify)	$	_____
Total Liabilities	$	_____

Net Worth	$	_____

Cash Flow Chart (In-Depth)

Income **Average Per Month**

	Husband	Wife
His W-2 from work		XXXX
Her W-2 from work	XXXX	
Investment and dividends		
Business income, K-1, partnerships		
Part-Time job		
Rental / room $board received		
Military Pension		
Social Security		
Bonuses		
Unemployment		
Child support / alimony		
Royalties, trusts, estates		
Other income (specify)		

Total   Total

Total income for household

Expenses **Average Per Month**

HOUSING

Rent/Mortgage	
2nd Mort / Equity Line	
Homeowners/Renter's Insurance	
Condo Fees/HOA Dues	
Maintenance	
Utilities	
Water/Sewer/Garbage	
Cable	
Internet	
Telephone	

Sub Total

Expenses
(Continued)

Average Per Month

FOOD

Groceries _____

Eating Out _____

Sub Total ▨

MEDICAL CARE

Insurance _____

Eye Care _____

Dentist _____

Prescriptions

Sub Total ▨

TRANSPORTATION

Car Payment #1 _____

Car Payment #2 _____

Auto Insurance _____

Registration and tags _____

Gas/oil _____

Maintenance/repairs _____

Public transportation/
　　　tolls/parking

Sub Total ▨

CHILD CARE

Day care _____

School tuition/supplies _____

Clothing _____

Activities/lessons _____

Child Support/Alimony
paid

Sub Total ▨

SAVINGS

Emergency _____

Investments

Sub Total ▨

Expenses
(Continued)

Average Per Month

DEBT
Loan Payment
_____
Mortgage
_____
Credit Card #1
_____
Credit Card #2
_____
Credit Card #3
_____
Other
| Sub Total |

INSURANCE PREMIUMS
Life
_____
Disability
_____
Personal Property
_____
Long Term Care
_____
Other
| Sub Total |

ENTERTAINMENT
Movies/Concerts/Theater
_____
Books/Magazines
_____
CD/Tapes/Videos
_____
Sports/Hobbies
_____
Vacation/Travel
_____
NetFlix
_____
Other
| Sub Total |

(continued)

Expenses
(Continued)   <u>**Average Per Month**</u>

MISCELLANEOUS

Country Club Dues   _____

Banking Fees   _____

Laundry/dry cleaning   _____

Union Dues   _____

Pet Care   _____

Holiday/Birthday Gifts   _____

Cell Phone   _____

Postage   _____

Cigarettes/Alcohol   _____

Church/Charity gifting   _____

Beauty/barber   _____

Cosmetics/Manicure   _____

Clothing/jewelry   _____

Spa Membership   _____

Guy dues   _____

Other   _____

Other   _____

Other   _____

Other   _____

Other   _____

Sub Total

Total Expenses

Cash Flow
(Income - Expenses)

Sample In Force Illustration

To whom it may concern:

Please provide the following information regarding the policy or policies listed below:

- The most recent annual statement
- A projection of policy values on a guaranteed basis
- A projection of policy values at the current interest rate credited, and current mortality and other variable costs charged, assuming the current planned premium is paid as scheduled
- A projection based on the premiums required to endow the contract at policy maturity at the current interest rate credited, and current mortality and other variable costs charged
- If this is a Variable policy, then show the subaccount performance at 0%, 5% and 7% gross
- Other: _____

Policy Owner	Date of Birth		Social Security Number
Address			Phone Number
City		State	ZIP
Insured	Date of Birth		Social Security Number
Policy Number(s)			

Please provide the documents via fax and US Mail to:

Name		Fax Number
Address		
City	State	ZIP

Should you need to reach me to discuss further, please call me at the number listed above:

Policy Owner Signature	Date

Glossary

401(k), 403(b), 457 plans: Employer sponsored retirement plans offered to eligible employees. Employees contribute income on a pre-tax basis. Some companies will match a certain percentage of contribution.

Asset allocation: Spreading your investments across different asset classes, such as stocks, bonds, CDs, and mutual funds. Through asset allocation, you generally lower your overall risk.

Assets: All the things that one owns.

Beneficiary: The person or persons you choose who will receive money or other benefits when you die. On contractual investments (like life insurance, retirement accounts, and annuities) and in trust documents, you name a beneficiary.

Brokerage firm: A company that is licensed to sell investments to the general public. These companies are governed by many agencies, including FINRA.

CERTIFIED FINANCIAL PLANNER™: A professional designation offered by the Certified Financial Planning Board of Standards. A person holding the CFP® must pass comprehensive educational classes in Financial Planning, Insurance Planning and Risk Management, Employee Benefits Planning, Estate Planning, Investment Planning, Income Tax, and Retirement Planning. The CFP practitioner must also agree to a high degree of ethical standards. Continuing education is required to maintain the CFP designation.

Chartered Financial Consultant (ChFC®): As the financial world became more complicated, the ChFC was created in 1982 to further enhance the insurance professional. As important as the CLU is, the ChFC takes the next step by including financial planning and wealth creation. The American College (www.theamericancollege.edu) confers this professional designation. The ChFC professional also has strict continuing educational requirements that must be met as well as professional standards of conduct combined with ethical training. Continuing education is required to maintain the ChFC designation.

Chartered Life Underwriter (CLU®): Designation established in 1927. The CLU professional is highly educated with a rigorous educational program, has required experience in the field, and can provide a wide range of financial planning and insurance expertise. The American College (www.theamericancollege.edu) confers this professional designation. Continuing education is required to maintain the CLU designation.

Disability income insurance: A type of insurance that pays some money to people who are injured or sick and cannot work. Payments are made each month. Disability plans can be either short-term or long-term. If you buy your own disability insurance, the benefits are free of income tax. If your employer pays for it, the benefits are taxable.

Diversification: See Asset allocation.

Durable Power of Attorney: A legally recognized document that allows an individual to grant permission to another to have the right to make decisions on his/her behalf. Once given, this power continues until revoked and can be used by your designee with or without your consent.

Estate planning documents: These are legally executed documents that define your estate plan. There are four documents in most estate plans: a will, a durable power of attorney, a health care directive, and a trust.

Financial advisor: A person you hire to help you manage your financial plan. Almost anyone can call themselves a financial advisor. There is little industry oversight as to the determination of what makes a person a financial advisor. The consumer should exercise caution as to the experience, expertise, knowledge, and credentials when hiring a financial advisor.

Joint Tenants with Rights of Survivorship (JTWROS): Legal title that is held by more than one person. All parties have rights to the money, and at the death of one of the owners, the remaining owner(s) receives the money. By "operation of law" this asset is immediately available to the joint owner regardless of the value. JTWROS assets are not governed by the will or the trust.

Living will: This allows you to state the types of life-sustaining medical care you want – or do not want – if you are unable to communicate those choices.

Titling: The important legal way an asset is owned. Do not underestimate the need to check on how you own your assets and adjust as needed how your accounts are titled.

Trust: A legal document where you name someone to manage designated assets in a trust. Setting up a living trust may be costly, but it can help protect assets in the trust from public disclosure and the probate process.

Viatical settlement or life settlement: A transaction where a person sells his or her life insurance policy to a company for a portion of its value. The amount of money paid often depends on life expectancy. The payment may range from 30% for someone with a life expectancy measured in years, to 80% for someone who has months to live.

Will: A legal document that says how and to whom your assets will be distributed after your death. If you die without a will (called "intestate"), your assets will be distributed according to the laws of the state you live in. The document used to name a legal guardian for your minor children or disabled adult child.

INDEX

Bibliography

Barney, Colleen, Esq., and Victoria Collins, PhD, CFP. *Best Intentions, Ensuring Your Estate Plan Delivers Both Wealth and Wisdom.* Chicago: Dearborn Trade Publishing, 2002.

Bove, Alexander, Jr. *The Complete Book of Wills, Estates & Trusts*, 3rd ed. New York: Owl Book, Henry Holt and Company, 2005.

Clifford, Denis. *Estate Planning Basics*, 3rd ed. Berkeley, CA: Nolo, 2005.

Cullen, Melanie with Shae Irving. *Get It Together: Organize Your Records So Your Family Won't Have To*, Nolo, 950 Parker Street, Berkeley, CA 94710, 2007

Lucal, Jane B. *Plan Now or Pay Later*. Princeton: Bloomberg Press, 2001

Scroggin, John J. AEP, JD, LL.M. and Donna Pagano CFP® *Family Love Letter*. www.familyloveletter.com

Resources

Arlington Benefits Group
Greg Clough
1100 North Glebe Road, Ste 1010
Arlington, VA 22201
703-224-8085
greg@arlbenefits.com
www.arlbenefits.com

Cantella & Co., Inc.
Two Oliver Street, 11th Floor
Boston, MA 02109
800-333-3502
www.Cantella.com

Family Love Letter
Donna Pagano, CFP®, President
3625 E Thousand Oaks Blvd
Suite 138
Westlake Village, CA 91362
805-497-7048
dpagano@familyloveletter.com
www.FamilyLoveLetter.com

William J Kovatch, Jr
Attorney at Law, P.L.L.C.
717 King Street, Suite 205
Alexandria, VA 22314
703-837-8832
info@kovatchelderlaw.com
www.KovatchElderLaw.com

Gura & Possessky, P.L.L.C.
Laura Possessky
1629 K Street, Suite 300
Washington, DC 20006
202-508-1055
laura@gurpossessky.com
www.gurapossessky.com

RebeccaPattonPhotography.com
RebeccaPattonPhotography@
cox.net
703-244-3313

Stitely & Karstetter, CPA
Frank Stitely, CPA, CVA
140616-D Sullyfield Circle
Chantilly, VA 20151
703-802-2309
fstitely@skcpas.com
www.skcpas.com

MJC Insurance Group
Matthew Crum
15918 Greymill Manor Drive
Haymarket, VA 20169
571-248-0253

60 Plus Association
    703-807-2070
    www.60plus.org

American Cancer Society
    800-ACS-2345
    www.cancer.org

American College (for ChFC® and CLU®)
    888-263-7265
    www.TheAmericanCollege.edu

Bloch Cancer Foundation
    800-433-0464
    www.BlochCancer.org

Cancer Legal Resource Center (CLRC)
    866-843-2572
    www.CancerLegalResourceCenter.org

Cancer Treatment Centers of America
    888-816-5122
    www.CancerCenter.com

Center for Disease Control and Prevention
    800-232-4636
    www.cdc.gov

Certified Financial Planner Board of Standards, Inc.
    800-487-1497
    www.cfp.net

Centers for Medicare & Medicaid Services (CMS) - HHS
800-633-4227
www.cms.hhs.gov

Department of Veterans Affairs
800-827-1000
www.va.gov

FINRA
301-590-6500
www.finra.org

Financial Planning Association
800-647-6340
www.fpanet.org

Internal Revenue Service (IRS)
800-829-1040
www.irs.gov

Life With Cancer®
703-698-2526
www.LifeWithCancer.org

LIVESTRONG®
www.LiveStrong.com

National Association of Personal Financial Advisors
800-366-2732
www.napfa.org

National Cancer Institute
800-422-6237 (800-4-CANCER)
www.cancer.gov

Our Journey of Hope
      888-399-8126
      www.OurJouneyOfHope.com
Smith Farm Center for Healing and the Arts
      202-483-5600
      www.SmithFarm.com

Social Security Administration
      800-772-1213
      www.socialsecurity.gov

About the Author

Shak Hill owns Lantern Wealth Management, LLC, a comprehensive wealth management company. A CERTIFIED FINANCIAL PLANNER™ practitioner, a Chartered Life Consultant, a Chartered Financial Consultant, Shak also holds a Masters Degree in Finance. He prides himself on taking time to explain the sometimes complicated financial world and making it easier to understand. He loves to teach and help enhance the overall level of understanding of financial planning and the importance of creating your unique financial plan.

An area of great concern is helping those who have been diagnosed with serious medical conditions, like cancer or a need for organ transplants. During this incredibly stressful and frightening time, Shak can help consolidate financial matters, simplify the financial web of accounts, statements and such, as well as ensure that you have proper estate planning documentation in place. Shak is an organ donor and on the national bone marrow transplant list. He donates blood every 56 days, without fail. He has been there; he has walked in your shoes; let him be of help to you and your family.

Shak and Robin raise six children (of which four are adopted) and over the last thirteen years, they have fostered twenty-four children.

Shak is interested in any feedback that you have regarding this book. He will personally responded to every comment.

A gifted speaker, Shak is available for presentations to your group about updated and timely financial topics. He can also be a key note speaker about working with the widow and the importance of understanding the challenges that she faces, also the importance of financial planning when the doctor says it's cancer or other life threatening diagnosis. If you are interested in working with Shak regarding your personal finances, feel free to contact him through his email address.

You can order additional copies on line at your favorite book web site. For bulk discounts, please feel free to contact Shak's office or visit his web site.

www.YourFinancialGuidingLight.com

Robak@YourFinancialGuidingLight.com

This material is not intended to provide legal, tax or investment advice, or to avoid penalties that may be imposed under U.S. Federal tax laws, nor is it intended as a complete discussion of the tax and legal issues surrounding retirement investing. Contact your tax advisor to learn more about the rules that may affect individual situations. Lantern Wealth Management, LLC does not provide legal or tax advice. For legal or tax advice, please seek the services of a qualified professional.

Invite Shak to be your next Guest Speaker

Shak enjoys public speaking and will be an excellent addition to any meeting. He can speak on a wide variety of financial topics.

Shak has a Masters Degree in Finance. He is a CERTIFIED FINANCIAL PLANNER™ practitioner, a Chartered Life Underwriter and a Chartered Financial Consultant. A former pilot in the US Air Force, Shak enjoys imparting knowledge and tackling the sometimes difficult financial topics with fun and easy to understand financial stories and real life examples to help all better understand the sometimes tricky financial topics.

You and your group will enjoy having Shak!

Make It a Great Day To Live!

Your Financial Guiding Light™

You can help make this book even better. Send your story, comments, corrections and suggestions to Robak@YourFinancialGuidingLight.com. Please put WDSIC (When Doctor Says It's Cancer) in the subject line.

LaVergne, TN USA
12 May 2010
182324LV00003B/33/P